just around yesterday's corne

a contemplation of the

TRAMWA...

and other historic 'ways'

IN AND AROUND

STOCKPORT

Reddish, August 1950

Photo: courtesy R.W.A. Jones

COMPILED and WRITTEN by

RAYMOND KEELEY

Copyright © 1990 by Foxline Publishing and R. Keeley

ISBN 1 870119 09 6

All rights reserved

Designed and edited by Gregory K. Fox
Typeset by Ryburn Typesetting Ltd, Luddendenfoot, Halifax
Printed by The Amadeus Press, Huddersfield

Published by Foxline Publishing
32, Urwick Road, Romiley, Stockport SK6 3JS

Below: Woodley, Hyde Road, c.1947. Car No. 10, en route for Hyde, pauses outside the Lowes Arms. The fare stage for this point was Bredbury St. Mark's Church, costing the passenger 2½d to travel from Mersey Square, or 6d for the full run to Hyde.

Acknowledgements

Although tramway systems have always fascinated me – especially those described in this book, the subject is not one on which I can claim to be an expert. As always, it is the 'memories' theme that claims my attention and, in this respect, I am perhaps in harmony with those who will browse through the following pages. It is a theme that has been basic to the many articles I have had published in various railway magazines and annuals, and in the few books on the subject of railways that have appeared under my name.

Obviously one cannot dream all the time! Therefore extensive research is essential for most writers dealing with a definite subject. For myself, that concerning tramway history required much study and investigation, and in this connection that ultimate historical and technical record, Maurice Marshalls Stockport Corporation Tramways book, has been constantly by my side. However, my approach to the subject – as in the railway writing, is of course quite different.

The purist might suggest that it is the romance rather than the reality that appeals to me – and so in that respect I have to agree. Perhaps it is a mixture of the two, although I do make an effort to present the historical/technical data as accurately as possible. Primarily, it was my desire to portray the Stockport, and for that matter the Manchester-tramcars, against the interesting background through which they operated. To this end I have, apart from the writing, relied heavily on some marvellous old postcards, together with the photographic achievements of those whose names are listed below.

Both my sons have helped. Michael, a deputy librarian at Manchester Central Library, by finding answers to some of the historical queries. Patrick, with valuable old postcards from his collection of Stockport views. Both have a wealth of knowledge related to the public transport scene. My thanks also to Miss Lynne Hamilton and Ros Lathbury of Stockport Libraries Local Studies section for helping with prints from the photographic archives and to the following whose photographs appear herein. John Fozard, Edward Gray, R.W.A. Jones, F.N.T. Lloyd Jones, J.H. Meredith, A.D. Packer, H.B. Priestley, D.F. Tee, F.E.J. Ward, R.J.S. Wiseman, I.A. Yearsley, and Mr R. Benton of the National Transport Museum for permission to use prints from the negatives of R.B. Parr.

A list of names can never adequately convey how fully one appreciates the response and help so willingly given. To all these people I am truly grateful.

Raymond Keeley,
    Woodsmoor, Stockport. May 1990.

Introduction

Tramcars, especially in the first decade of this century, were a novel and perhaps, as seen through the eyes of local people, a rather dramatic addition to the mainly horse drawn vehicles on the roads of that time. Not surprisingly therefore, the area of St Peters Square, a tramway terminal point, became a popular venue for the postcard photographer in these pre-1914 days. There was also, among others, a further focal point in the shape of that popular place of entertainment, the imposing Theatre Royal. However, the predominant theme in this photograph is of course the tramcar, particularly that rather radiant example in the centre of the picture.

Stockport car No. 60 (from the 51–60 series built 1920/21) is on the St Peters Square to Hazel Grove service, and later, in the mid 1930s, given the service number 4A. This series of cars included, when built, the addition of platform doors and were the first totally enclosed cars in the fleet, initially being known as the Glasshouses. However, the innovation didn't last long, the doors being removed at the first overhaul or repaint. Perhaps the radiance is due to a repaint because, as far as I can make out, the doors appear to have been removed. Both the conductor – who seems to be about to reverse the trolley pole, and the driver, are obviously aware of the photographers presence.

The four wheeled Manchester car on the left is numbered, I think, 725 from a series built 1912/13. The route No. 35 would at that time be St Peters Square–Piccadilly Manchester using the circular pattern from Mersey Square (see also caption 73).

The buildings between the Imperial Hotel and St Peters Chambers, which included Goodalls tailors shop, were demolished to allow for the extension of Piccadilly to St Peters Square. Behind the statue of Richard Cobden is Hidderleys, the decorators, whose premises were demolished in 1976.   *Photo: E. Gray*

Evolving Patterns and Historic 'ways'

Consider for a few moments the thrill, the anticipation of 'how it was' surrounding the activity of an archeological 'dig', strange stones and symbols unearthed in far off mystical lands and sands. Or, come closer to home, to behold stonework weathered by distant centuries, shaped by craftsmen from long forgotten generations. Each and all a revelation of long hidden secrets from the past ages of mankind. We marvel, and rightly so, at the creativity of peoples who lived maybe just a few centuries ago, or in an age so distant their existence seems concealed in a shroud of time. We marvel because the stones, the pottery, the metalwork etc, were fashioned by human hands and thus, through human imagination.

Yet, as impressive as such human achievement may be, the 'dig' to uncover quarry stone, build a railway, or more recently in Stockport, a motorway, reveals in perhaps even more dramatic fashion, evidence of the wonder of the earth's past ages, so remote as to make the arrival of literate mankind seem but yesterday! Then can spark in our minds the additional eternal questions, the 'how and why' of earths order, pattern – plan?

Thus the 19th and 20th century observer has had a chance to glimpse the size structure and substance of strata concealed by time unimaginable. Stockport has had its share of such momentous structural revelation, both through the efforts of man and, across the ages, by the evolving efforts of nature in the form of the rivers and valleys. From the South Pennine area known as the Peak District there flows a countless trickle of tiny waterways which in turn become the streams that make and feed the rivers of the region. Rivers which, though they may have fond memories for many of us, do not perhaps merit the adjective 'great' – well, at least not until they reach towards an eastern or western sea outlet. It is in the form of the great tidal estuaries – Mersey and Humber, which offered a means of sea transportation to distant lands, that the wider mantle of fame descends. Never the less, our northern rivers do have a claim to local fame since, in the early decades of the industrial revolution (18th and 19th century) they did provide a source of power for the mills of Lancashire, Cheshire, and Derbyshire, and as impressive reservoirs in the river valleys bear witness, a vital supply source for water. Paradoxically, those same river valleys helped create some of the barriers and obstacles that bedevilled mans efforts to transport his ilk by road and track and, in more recent times, as evidenced by spectacular viaducts, posed major headaches for the builders of our railways. The rivers, the valleys, even the viaducts that add their own measure of majesty and character, how unimaginably lifeless and barren our northern lands would be without them..

4. Marple: Goyt Viaduct, 26th April 1984. South of Marple, at a point where the valley narrows and the river wriggles against a tough layer of glacial debris; there strides – in graceful fashion, the Goyt Viaduct. It was built in the early 1860s to carry the railway known as The Marple, New Mills and Hayfield Junction (amalgamated into the Manchester, Sheffield and Lincolnshire Railway within five days of its opening) – railway company names changed over the years but the viaduct goes soldiering on! The octagonal shaped house in the foreground was built I believe about 1801 for the use of the keeper of the nearby weir, flood gates etc, which controlled the flow of water to the main reservoir (Roman Lakes) of Mellor Mill – doubtless a highly responsible job that required constant surveillance. The whole area is fascinating to explore, for those interested in Industrial Archaeology. *Photo: R. Keeley*

2. Reddish Vale, 7th March 1975. Well known to me in my teenage days as the '16 arches', though only 6 show in the photograph, Reddish Vale and the railway viaduct was a popular venue for a school friend and I. Steam trains, the grace and elegance of the viaduct, the magic of the river and footpaths, what more could one have wished for.

The river in the photograph – The Tame, has about a couple of miles to go before joining the River Goyt near the bottom of Lancashire Hill where, together they become The Mersey. The viaduct carries the railway from Romiley Junction to Ashburys, a line jointly operated by the Midland, and Manchester, Sheffield and Lincolnshire companies, and opened for traffic in 1875. At the grouping of railways in 1923 it became the preserve of the LMSR and LNER although Midland and Great Central locomotives could still be seen until the last days of steam. *Photo: R. Keeley*

3. Heaton Mersey, 6th April 1972. The viaduct in the foreground carries the erstwhile Midland Railway direct line (New Mills South Junction to Heaton Mersey – completed in 1902) across the River Mersey. The Cheshire Lines route from Woodley Junction to Skelton Junction, running from east to west, crosses the river on the viaduct seen in the background. Both viaducts are now demolished that carrying the Midland lines in 1974, and the Cheshire Lines as recently as 1986. It was sad to see them go, particularly the elegant pathway arches of the Cheshire Lines viaduct, with their graceful multi curves in brick and stone. What a contrast to the bleak brash motorway bridge of today. *Photo: R. Keeley*

Stockport
A meeting of the 'ways' – water, road, rail

Around the northern and eastern edges of what might be described as land formed into a shallow half bowl are the groups of hills and sometimes frowning escarpment that peer towards a central area. Then, nestling on the lower slopes and valley bottoms dividing the hills are the towns which, making a rough semi circle, gaze, perhaps at times quizzically, in the same direction, since they are all part of the Greater Manchester conurbation. Most are astride or adjacent to a river, primarily for reasons historical as mentioned previously. I would doubt however if any could claim to be more dramatically situated than Stockport, located as it is at the southern end of the arc.

The town is at a focal point or conflux of a whole fan of waterways converging from the western edge of the South Pennine uplands. These, given variously the title of brook or stream, progressively form and flow into three major water courses, each large enough to be entitled the description river.

The River Tame, whose source is on the far away Standedge/Saddleworth moors – that watershed between Lancashire and Yorkshire, finds a tortuous way that intersects the townships of Stalybridge and Ashton and finally meets the River Goyt at Stockport. Meanwhile, the Goyt, flowing down from the high moorland west of Buxton, had been joined, in rather more picturesque surroundings at Marple, by the River Etherow, the source of the latter being shrouded in those grim but grand deep recesses of Longdendale.

Thus, unobtrusively, except when the storms do blow, two major rivers join harmoniously beneath the thunder of a motorway and, becoming one, take the illustrious name, Mersey. But oh what irony the fates bestow. For at this very spot the grandeur that should be vanishes, then does indignity mock the singing waters as they are channelled through a man made concrete trough. There it is desecrated, and in full view for those who choose to stride a few yards from where the tinned foods and glassed jars rattle across the massed checkout ranks.

Urbane maybe, yet at this place in long ages past, a mailed fist of determined – and perhaps unimaginably turbulent water, further activated by rain frost and ground erosion, made contact with a final, low lying but tough, outlier of the Pennine ridges, this being a north to south ridge of Permian sandstone. The water, after countless twists and turns, found the beginnings of a weak point in the structure, cracks or crevice that would be eroded and, in the primaeval struggle, eventually battered its way through to find release across the north Cheshire plain and into the Irish Sea.

The long ages of turmoil and earth shaking conflict left in its wake a sandstone bluff on the south side of the river. This would be an obvious place for a fortified point – as indeed it became, a prime necessity for area domination and control down the ages, and as such requiring the 'ways' of communication to be easily available and pass within view.

The primary lines of communication in northern England have long been north/south in direction, aiming generally towards our

continued over

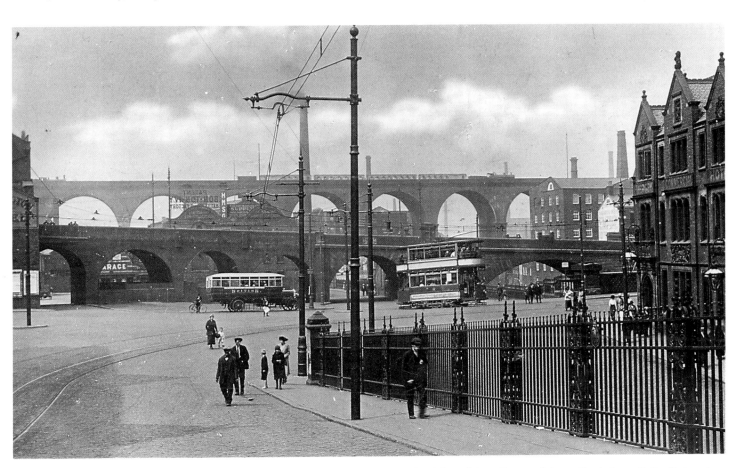

5. Mersey Square, c.1920. Though the river is concealed – beneath the road arch to the right and the railway arch immediately beneath the first carriage and locomotive tender of the train, this was, and still is, a dramatic view of one 'meeting of the 'ways''.

The bus, solid tyres, is I believe one that was operated by the British Automobile Traction Company, based in Macclesfield and working into Stockport by an agreement made in 1920 with the Corporation. From the pole in the centre of the picture the wires of the trackless trolley system are suspended. This gave vehicles access to the depot from the systems terminus in St Peters Square. The tram is about to proceed through the arch under Wellington Road, towards Brinksway, on the Cheadle and Gatley route.

ancient capital London, and that southern coast that twice saw long term invasion (Roman/Norman), both setting greater imprint on a natural direction of communications. So it could be expected that at least one major track or roadway from Manchester, a north west centre of population and commerce over the centuries, would inevitably follow an established route in that south/south easterly direction and, for practical reasons, attempt to pass through other smaller centres of population and trade activity. Therefore it seems logical that a place six miles to the south which had grown around a confluence of rivers would figure prominently on such a route.

So it came about that an ancient way would pass precipitously – or so it probably seemed in early days – down the eastern shoulder of that aforementioned ridge of sandstone, we still call it Lancashire Hill, and cross the river at the place that became known as Lancashire Bridge. As the textile trade of Stockport thrived and expanded in the 18th and early 19th centuries, so the route, along Underbank and Hillgate in a southerly direction, became more established as an important thoroughfare and the life and business activity of the town grew around it.

Then, in 1824, an act of parliament was to have a far reaching and quite dramatic impact on the layout of the town. The act provided for an important new road to be built and, in what must have seemed an innovation for those days, it would by-pass the old town centre to the west. Three and a quarter miles long and completed in 1826 and, being named after the victor of Waterloo, it

became Wellington Road north/south according to which side of the River Mersey it lay, extending from its junction with Manchester Road in Heaton Chapel to the junction of Buxton Road/Bramhall Lane. Doubtless it is one of the earliest examples of a major traffic route being lifted to the edge of a town centre and, in the process, traversing what, at that time, would be partially a rural area.

The unusual effect this had at Stockport, as compared to other towns where by-pass or road widening came as the motorised age developed, has resulted in the street pattern of old town remaining largely intact and retaining a separate importance. Most of the public and other major buildings of the Victorian period gradually spread alongside the new road and as a result there is a very clear distinction between the old and new town centres which, to a degree, now seem to compliment each other.

The opportunity the new road offered for developing the main direction of traffic movement was clear to see and, as the age of mass public transport by road began to dawn at the end of the Nineteenth Century, it became obvious it would play a vital part. Thus, with the coming of the electric tramway age, after a brief period of horse drawn trams, Wellington Road became a key to the layout of the system and Mersey Square a spacious fulcrum as it gradually evolved. The resultant layout made for a basically north/south, east/west system, indeed, an aerial view might see it as a giant cross with Mersey Square as the centre.

Mersey Square – a spacious fulcrum

6. Mersey Square, c.1913. The postmark on the back of this card is, so far as I can make out, 1913. The imposing tramway office block, seen just above the roof of the covered top car, had been completed just four years previously. The tram depot, as it existed before the extension of 1929, is to the right and behind the office block, on the edge of the river.

The covered top car is travelling from the Cheadle direction and has just passed under the arch below Wellington Road. The open top car, which appears perilously close to colliding with the horse drawn van, will be stationary, allowing the covered car time to clear the interlaced track beneath the arch.

7. Princes Street, c.1912. A view looking down Princes Street from its junction with Wellington Road, the Touchstone Inn being prominent in the left foreground. The street is crowded and people appear to wander freely. The two lads in right foreground are pulling a handcart with another giving assistance at the rear. As far as I can make out the open top car is No. 29 – one of the original batch of 30 cars. It was rebuilt in the early 1920s with top cover, vestibule platforms, but open balcony ends. Renumbered 64 in 1944, it lasted until December 1950.

8. Wellington Road/Princes Street, c.1928. An interesting view taken from a slightly different angle to the previous one. The date, I think, would be late 1920s. The tram track in the foreground leads into Heaton Lane Depot, opened in January 1924. The building on the corner of Princes Street/Wellington Road South, appears to be a rebuild of the corner building seen on the previous illustration. This whole block of property was demolished in 1934 when the Mersey Square area was extended, the latter being part of the scheme that involved building a new bridge across the river and the beginnings of the construction of Merseyway.

9. Wellington Road. This I would suggest is a late 1930s view. The Touchstone Inn is in evidence on the left and seems to have had something of a facelift when compared with the 1912 facade. On the right are the new tram offices opened in 1927. They were not a replacement for the Mersey Square offices which remained, but in more limited use. The three trams are too distant to identify but doubtless the car on the left is en route for Cheadle Heath, the other two possibly being for Hazel Grove and Manchester respectively.

10. Mersey Square Depot, 15th January 1950. A glance into Mersey Square Depot, with car No. 80 centre, and car No. 8 to the right. The enclosed section of the platform on car No. 8 was known as a 'plant on' vestibule (a form of what we might now consider to be prefabrication). It could be quickly and easily positioned and give cover on the platform for both passengers and the driver when he was operating from that end of the car. Looking back from our own age of somewhat cushioned comfort, at least where transport is concerned, it probably seems quite strange that tram drivers, particularly in the earlier decades of the century, could be so unprotected from the elements – rain, snow, wind. But of course, it was a form of punishment, for being working class, and cheerfully accepted by the innocents who drove tram cars, horse wagons and drays. To say nothing of the many thousands of steam locomotives still around in those days, that offered the barest minimum of protection for the train crews. In the case of tram car No. 8 built 1901, the 'plant on' vestibule didn't arrive until rather late in its life – 1937!

Photo: J.H. Meredith

11. Mersey Square, c.1949. Car No. 72 about to proceed towards the interlaced double track section beneath the arch under Wellington Road South. This car was one of the 66–75 series ordered in 1922 and, with the exception of 69, a vehicle badly damaged in an accident on Chestergate in 1950, all remained in service until closure of the system in Stockport. Merseyway is to the left of the picture.

Photo: J. Fozard

12. Mersey Square, May 1949. The ornate tram depot frontage of 1929, complete with name (Corporation of Stockport Tramway Depot) and coat of arms virtually sculptured into the stonework. Indeed, a visual asset to the area around the Square – I doubt we would take such trouble today! The photograph underlines the somewhat more carefree way people could stroll across the roads of those days, when traffic was light and moved at a more humane pace. Albeit, you can still stroll in Mersey Square today – but you perhaps need to skip more quickly across the busways! *Photo: D.F. Tee*

13. Mersey Square, May 1949. Car No. 30 in Mersey Square and probably en route to Reddish. Originally Car No. 1, it was renumbered No. 30 in 1944. The photograph shows the right hand reverse spiral staircase as built into the original batch of 30 cars, and retained by 10 of them. Later batches of cars had left hand ascending spiral staircases. Part of the Touchstone Inn and the famous UCP tripe shop can be seen on the left of the photograph, on the site now occupied by Debenhams.
Photo: D.F. Tee

Dine in the "Oak Room"

The rendezvous of all people who enjoy good food and the most handsomely designed Cafe-Restaurant in the North of England, where smart and courteous service is the accompaniment of satisfying meals

LUNCHEONS 1/-, 1/3, 1/6, 1/9, 2/3   TEAS 10d. to 2/-

Stockport Co-operative Society
CHESTERGATE, STOCKPORT   LIMITED

Gx 9640

Crossley Road	S.C.T.	Woods-moor Lne
Heaton Moor Rd.	Issued subject to the Corp'ration By-laws	Dialstone Lane
Mersey Square	Available only on Car issued.	Hazel Grove Ter
Gatley Terminus		Northgate Road
Cheadle Heath S'n	FARE	Houldsworth Arms
Bound'ry Bridge	3d	Greg Street
Mersey Square	This Ticket must be shewn for inspection when required.	Reddish Terminus
...ley Terminus		Bredbury Station
St. Peters gate	given up on demand.	Woodley Station

Williamson, Printer, Ashton.

Clatter on the stones!

Before the arrival of the electric tramway era at the turn of the century, Stockport enjoyed a brief period of horse trams, albeit that the route pattern was quite modest in form. A line north, operational from 1881, ran from St Peters Square into Manchester Piccadilly and was operated by the Manchester Carriage and Tramways Company. In 1889, the Stockport and Hazel Grove Carriage and Tramway Company came into being and was authorised to construct a line from St Peters Square to Hazel Grove, opening in 1890 with a terminus adjacent to the Bulls Head Hotel on Torkington Road. There was also a short branch along Greek Street and Castle Street terminating at Grenville Street.

By comparison with the horse buses they replaced, the horse trams were seen as a great improvement although I imagine both forms of transport seem primitive when compared to the cushioned comfort enjoyed by todays more mobile society! Nevertheless, the move from cobbled road to smooth rail was bound to enhance the quality of riding, with smoother running, less shaking and jolting, and faster – though that probably meant a mere seven or eight miles an hour instead of five or six!

A Salford newspaper in 1877, describing the opening of a new horse tramway in Salford, commented on the smooth roll of the cars compared to the noisy jolting movement of the buses – delicate ladies could now glide to town without the danger of headache or sickness while the elderly could now ride with a measure of comfort undreamed of in their youth.

With the iron bound wheels of the horse buses clattering across the stone setts, shaking and jolting would seem almost an understatement, and it is hard to imagine that the wooden seating and early form of suspension would do very much to enhance the rough nature of the ride. The discomfort of such a form of travelling would probably be accentuated by the style of dress then fashionable, and perhaps in particular for members of the fairer sex encumbered with the tight fitting garments, ankle length dress and corsetry etc, of the time. Boarding or dismounting from the bus would, presumably, be somewhat awkward. How precarious for either sex, climbing a rather exposed curving stairway to the upper, open top deck, with a slender handrail to save you toppling to the street below, this applying to the horse trams as well. Then, on wintry days, to meet wind or rain, with perhaps one hand steadying head gear that only lightly rested on both male or female heads, I wonder how many top hats were whisked away in such conditions?

Horse trams were clearly more comfortable, though the rate of progression was of course still quite slow and still punctuated by an aroma from the exhaust end of the motive power. This at least though would have a certain wholesome quality reminiscent of the farmyard, and quite unlike the insidious reek of petrol fumes from modern forms of mechanised energy.

The horse trams were short lived, for it seemed that time was running out for them almost from the beginning. An era we know as the Victorian period was drawing to a close and doubtless then – as at the end of the 1980s, there was a certain looking forward to the beginning of a new century – and wondering. A strange sensing and perhaps expectation of change and an enhanced awareness of time and history in transition.

Perhaps people find a certain mystique, something symbolic about the years that turn around the pinnacle of a century. Certainly the years that turned the end of the 19th into the 20th century would have appeared at the time, almost sensational where they concerned public street transport. They were the years that heralded the beginning, the grandeur, and the rapid development of the electric tramways, when local pageantry and celebration heralded the opening of each new section of the lines. Perhaps no other century had ever opened quite so dramatically, a portend, it seemed, for the brief halcyon, high spirited years of the Edwardian period that were to follow.

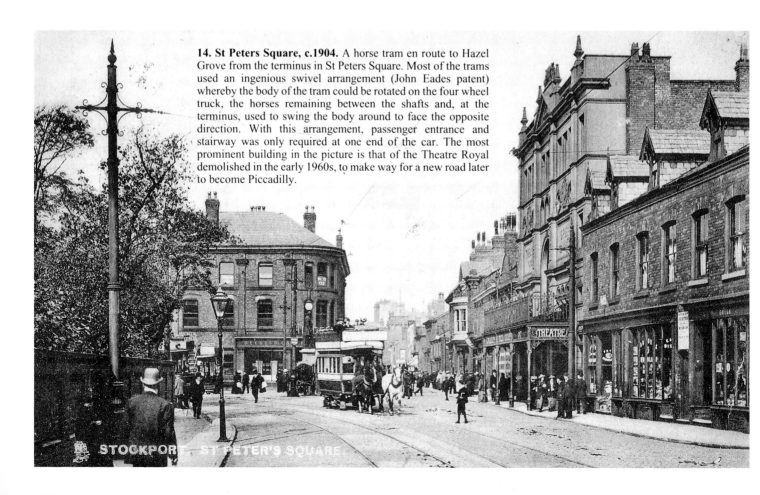

14. St Peters Square, c.1904. A horse tram en route to Hazel Grove from the terminus in St Peters Square. Most of the trams used an ingenious swivel arrangement (John Eades patent) whereby the body of the tram could be rotated on the four wheel truck, the horses remaining between the shafts and, at the terminus, used to swing the body around to face the opposite direction. With this arrangement, passenger entrance and stairway was only required at one end of the car. The most prominent building in the picture is that of the Theatre Royal demolished in the early 1960s, to make way for a new road later to become Piccadilly.

STOCKPORT. ST PETER'S SQUARE

15. St Petersgate, c.1904. St Petersgate as depicted on an early postcard. The tram, pulled by three horses is en route to Hazel Grove, horse trams operating this route until 1905. The extra horse was necessary on the uphill section when the tram turned onto Wellington Road South. The single track at this point was also used by Manchester's, then new, electric cars, as evidenced by the overhead power wires. At this time Manchester cars operated on the Manchester/Stockport service and from Mersey Square they worked in a circular fashion up Daw Bank to St Peters Square, and then along St Petersgate before turning into Wellington Road South and back to Mersey Square. Prominent on the left is a corner of the Unitarian Church and beyond, the bold and decorative front of the Stockport Central Baths which was remodelled in 1950.

16. Wellington Road South. This postcard is postmarked 1904. The horse tram on the right (only two horses) is en route from Hazel Grove back to St Petersgate, while the Hansom cab in the foreground probably conveys a more affluent member of society to town. Prominent on the left is the frontage of the Brookfield Hotel, the name and datestone (1898) being still a noticeable feature of this building. Further along, the few shops – long disappeared, stand approximately at the point where Longshut lane was widened. Beyond, the cupola like towers of Trinity Methodist Church act as a local landmark.

17. Buxton Road. An unused postcard and therefore without a date/postmark, but clearly of similar vintage to the views of the previous two cards. Today, eighty odd years later, the building line on the left – a focal point in this district known as Heaviley, appears to have changed very little. The large trees on the left have gone, replaced by a form of shop frontage against the old building. The Duke of York Hotel remains and visually unaltered. Other housing further along has become shop premises. The houses seen on the right hand edge of the card have long been demolished. The horse tram and cyclist dominate the foreground of what appears a very quiet road. Indeed the main change, if you stand on the same spot as that photographer of nearly ninety years ago, is the ceaseless cacaphony of present day traffic on the A6!

Just a few lines

The constructional powers granted to Stockport Corporation in 1899 allowed for a basic electric tramway system to emerge in 1900 and followed by further extensions in 1902, a system that, along with those developed in other towns, may seem comparatively sparse when compared to the complex interlacing of bus routes familiar to us today.

The problem of course was the infrastructional paraphernalia surrounding that most grand and ostentatious of street vehicles. Rigid steel wheels on rigid steel track required great attention to the stability of road surfaces, and the motive power supply required substantial metal poles at frequent intervals plus a complex interlace of power wiring. Clearly the costs for installation and maintenance would be heavy, so therefore the decision to construct a tram route would have been fraught with anxieties concerning need and viability. No doubt the desire of men in high public office to best serve their community would be in constant tangle with an equivalent concern about costs and the return on capital outlay.

However, in the fullness of time, lines were built and some main routes came into contact or joint operation with systems operating in other nearby towns. Eventually, in what we know as the Greater Manchester area, a considerable web of tram routes emerged, and long distances could sometimes be covered sitting in that magical end section of the semi enclosed upper deck of some earlier cars – sometimes known as, riding on the outside.

The western and southernmost extension of the tramlines remained terminal at Gatley and Hazel Grove respectively, and, in terms of that return on capital outlay, it is difficult to envisage how, at least in the early part of this century, it could have been otherwise, the land to the south and west of those places being mostly rural, with decades to go past before the great outer urban expansion to the south of Stockport and Manchester.

By 1902 a through line to Hyde had been achieved, the operating responsibility for the venture being shared by Stockport Corporation and The Oldham, Ashton and Hyde Electric Tramway Ltd, with the company cars operating to Bredbury only and Stockport cars running through between Mersey Square and Hyde. There were some initial difficulties concerning low traffic density between Hyde and Bredbury and as a result it was decided that the route should be split, both undertaking choosing to make Pole Bank their terminus. This brought angry and vociferous public outcry – letters to the press etc, which, it would seem were effective in making sure the situation would not last long (2nd May–10th August 1903). Would be passengers were obviously concerned at having to change trams in what was then a fairly bleak spot at an altitude of 400ft; and doubtless were considering the problems the forthcoming winter might present, especially if waiting time between trams was involved, perhaps without shelter. So, public outcry, even at that time, did sometimes have an effect – after the 10th August through running from the Stockport end resumed. By 1925 the line had become jointly operated by Stockport Corporation tramways and what, through the aquiring of the company by various local authorities, was now known as S.H.M.D. Joint Board (Stalybridge, Hyde, Mossley, Dukinfield). Joint operation remained until May 1945, when it was agreed between the operators that owing to the condition of the S.H.M.D. cars (which were known affectionately as the 'Green Linnets' due to the dark green and cream livery) Stockport cars would now provide the complete service. Sadly, the through route with tram operation had less than two years to go, lasting only until March 1947.

The main route from Stockport into Manchester via Wellington Road/Stockport Road was, for its first 21 years, operated by Manchester cars, this being the result of an agreement between the Stockport and Manchester Corporations, and the intervening urban districts of Heaton Norris and Levenshulme. Finally, in 1924 (by which time Stockport and Manchester now had a common boundary at Lloyd Road, Levenshulme) a new agreement allowed for joint running between Stockport Corporation Tramways and the aspiring giant that was Manchester Corporation Tramways.

18. Buxton Road. Looking north, the view dates, I would think, from just pre 1914. The entrance to Davenport Park on the left, Corbar Road on the right. The present day roadside view from this point has not greatly changed, though the trees and foliage are perhaps somewhat thinner and less luxuriant.

19. Mersey Square, c.1910. Date stamped 1912 on the reverse side, this postcard view presents an interesting study of people walking and cycling in somewhat carefree fashion against a fascinating backdrop of buildings. Car No. 14, on the left, is en route to Gatley. The right hand reverse staircase, a feature of the first series of cars, can clearly be seen. To the right of the picture a Manchester car ascends Daw Bank, the Rock buildings dominating even in those days.

Thus, in the course of time (and perhaps such a phrase underlines most human systems of organisation which are usually subject to follow a course of constant change, revision and, hopefully, improvement, as ideas and technology develop) complex financial and working arrangements concerning responsibility for track and overhead wiring and their maintenance, the use and provision of cars, the apportioning of traffic receipts etc, passed gradually through their ordered ways of committee room procedure and agreement. What might be described as intensive 'behind the scenes' activity, with the intention of solving the wide range of problems that arise when considering a joint public transport operation. Activity that ultimately resulted in Stockport cars running through to Hyde and, later, S.H.M.D. cars into Stockport.

However, perhaps the most visual and dramatic result of such 'activity' was that which ultimately provided for joint running that would bring Stockport cars into the heart of Manchester and Manchester cars to the edge of open country at Hazel Grove! Indeed, if prestige be the name of the game, what could have been more satisfying for the Stopfordian than to see the cars with the Vermillion livery penetrate the inner fastness of the great Cottonopolis when, in sight and sound, they made their presence felt in Albert Square, Piccadilly, and in full view of Exchange Station and the Cathedral!

Of the remaining Stockport lines, one lengthy stretch veered away at the eastern end of Princes Street, up Lancashire Hill then in a northerly direction to find further contact with Manchester cars at Reddish (Bulls Head), a point that remained a terminus for Stockport cars from the south and Manchester cars from the north on normal services. This route, plus a short stretch along Greek Street/Castle Street and the lines to Cheadle and Gatley, completed the system in Stockport. Other proposed extensions that may have been in view never came to fruition.

When contemplating the lines to Cheadle and Gatley, one might wonder what prompted the decision to go ahead, especially as the

country beyond the first mile or so out of Stockport could be considered fairly rural, as indeed it was before the turn of the century. There were however certain land developments emerging and, like the route to Reddish, there was an additional factor that was likely to have some influence on any final decision to lay the lines, the presence of water!

Water – the key? A canal in one case, a river in the other. Both of these 'ways' offered essential services to industry, whether it be for navigation, or a ready source of power for water wheels, steam driven machinery, etc.

After reaching the crest of the long grind that is Lancashire Hill the tramway to Reddish was never, throughout the remainder of its length, at any great distance from the Stockport Branch of the Ashton Canal. Near the top of the Hill, the trams passed close to the basin where the canal terminated, on the brink, so the speak, of the great gap that forms the Mersey Valley. The tramway then veered away eastward along Sandy Lane before curving in a more northerly direction along Reddish and Gorton Roads, and roughly parallel but east of the canal.

Mills great and small varied in manufacturing processes but with textiles predominating, lined this section of the canal, especially at the southern end. What an impressive parade they made for the walker on the towpath; and dominating all, at least in my eyes, the magnificent Broadstone Mill. This mill, graced by two imposing chimneys and two elaborately decorated and domed water towers that would have enobled any cathedral, plus the Houldsworth Mill – still in situ as a building – were landmarks for miles around. Mills of such size would employ a large workforce, living nearby and in close proximity to Reddish Road and therefore a lucrative source of passenger traffic for the new tramway, the latter being extended section by section and completed to the Bulls Head by late 1903.

Significantly, the first mile or so of the route towards Cheadle would traverse Chestergate/Brinksway and quite literally hug the southern bank of the River Mersey, a length of the river which played host to several large textile mills and other sites of industrial activity, therefore large areas of employment and, again, a potential source of passengers and revenue and probably a strong influence in the decision to construct a tramway to the west of the town.

Onward to Cheadle Heath the road enters an area where, at the turn of the century, something different, in the form of potential industrial/commercial expansion, was in process of developing. The Midland Railway was now nearing the end of construction on a new railway between New Mills South Junction and Heaton Mersey. This would give a more direct route into Manchester Central Station and allow for further development of a competitive express train service between London and Manchester.

The new line, opened in 1902, involved the building of a tunnel at Disley (2½ miles long) and a massive viaduct across the river just south of Heaton Mersey Station. It also included a brand new five platformed station at Cheadle Heath that would provide a local service of trains to Manchester Central Station and, close by, a large goods shed and yards, plus extensive carriage sidings. In the Mersey Valley nearby, a large engine shed – Heaton Mersey, established in 1889 to serve other lines already existing, providing a further source of work for the local population.

These topographical changes to what, nearly a century ago, would be a mainly rural area, are perhaps hard to imagine today, but to the local people of the time they must have appeared monumental. Obviously the area was likely to expand in terms of population, and such growth was likely to spread to nearby Cheadle – already an established meeting point of roads from north and south as well as east and west.

It all seemed a further underline of that pivotal point between the end of one century and the beginning of the next. The sense of turning a corner with anticipation of great changes in the offing. Indeed, perhaps the new tramway, opened in sections – Brinksway/Cheadle Heath 1902/3 and finally to Gatley in early 1904, was almost a foregone conclusion.

As a tailpiece to my brief revue of Stockport Tramways, reference must be made to the trackless system which operated on a route from St Petersgate via Churchgate and Hall Street to Offerton Fold. The 'trackless trams' as they were called, were, in effect, an early form of trolleybus, single decked and with solid rubber tyres. An intricate overhead wiring system (German in origin and unique in this country) with a flexible cable and carriage attachment (known locally as the 'monkey') between the car and the overhead wires powered each car.

The system worked on a single pair of wires suspended one above the other (one supplying current the other acting as a return) and mainly along the easterly side of the route. Because of the single wiring system the carriage attachments on each vehicle could not pass each other; therefore it was necessary for the complete attachment to be switched from one to the other at the place where they would pass. This was usually near the Victoria Hotel on Hall Street. Obviously a tricky operation (and perhaps impractical in terms of route extensions), requiring the unplugging of the 'monkey' from the bulkhead of the outward bound vehicle, and replugging to the inward bound car, and vice versa.

The life of the system was brief (1913–1920), halted by the lack of spare parts for the three vehicles that operated the route, the latter then being taken over by petrol driven buses.

20. Hall Street, c.1913. Stockport's early form of trolleybus which operated on the system, unique in this country, described in the above chapter. Only three buses operated the route, St Petersgate–Offerton Fold, the one in the above view being No. 3. On the left is the Victoria Hotel, this being the usual passing point for the trolley buses and where the power attachment was switched between vehicles. The service was inaugurated on 10th March 1913 and it is possible that this old postcard, which appears to date from about that time, may have been issued to celebrate the event.

Tramways to Hazel Grove

21. Hazel Grove, c.1905. The original Hazel Grove terminus at Torkington Road. The postcard from which this view was taken is postmarked July 12th 1905 and, since the electric trams had only just replaced the horse trams (the newly electrified route, Stockport–Hazel Grove, was only inspected and opened for use on July 5th) it may well have been issued to commemorate this significant happening. Car No. 33 would be brand new, being of the 31–40 series which were ordered from the British Thompson Houston Company for the opening of the Hazel Grove and Edgeley lines. The ten cars comprising the series – and costing £618 each, being brought into commission in July 1905. Certainly there is an air of celebration, with a large crowd of people seen in the distance opposite the houses in this view towards Stockport.

22. Hazel Grove, c.1950. The car in this photograph is in roughly the same position as the rear car in the above photograph – except that about forty five years separate them! So not quite a 'then and now', since we are now almost another forty years or so further on in time. The name Bulls Head Hotel can clearly be seen through the tree branches. The Stockport Corporation bus and the North Western single decker (Bristol L5G), add further period atmosphere to the photograph.

Photo: F.N.T. Lloyd Jones

23. Hazel Grove, c.1948. The road junction at the Rising Sun – Buxton to the left, Macclesfield to the right, became the southernmost extension of the tramline after just an extra 198 yards from the original terminus at Torkington Road were completed in 1911. Car No. 76 is ready to move back over the crossing points. Faintly seen above the tram is the system of power wiring that could be used to allow the trolley pole to move in circular fashion as the car reversed. Then, when at a right angle to the car, a further quarter circle movement allowed the pole to come into a complete reverse position.

Photo: J. Fozard

24. Hazel Grove, c.1948. Driver and conductor pose for the photographers as car No. 78 stands poised for the journey to Crossley Road. After closure of the last through service to Manchester in January 1949, Stockport cars continued to operate a service between Hazel Grove and Crossley Road until this also ceased in January 1950.

Photo: F.N.T. Lloyd Jones

25. Hazel Grove, c.1948. London Road, with car No. 80 just a few hundred yards away from the terminus. As always, the buildings and shops of forty years ago make a fascinating study. *Photo: F.N.T. Lloyd Jones*

26. Buxton Road. In this view looking towards Stockport, car No. 75 is en route to Hazel Grove. The lorry on the left, proceeding north, gives an approximation of the entrance to Davenport Park. This late 1940s view makes an interesting comparison with the old postcard view in plate 18.

Photo: F.N.T. Lloyd Jones

27. Davenport, 4th May 1959. The south end of Davenport Station looking towards Hazel Grove, with the train, the 5.50pm Manchester London Road to Buxton, awaiting departure. The engine is 42887, a type that railway buffs would know as a 'Horwich Mogul', a mixed traffic engine although not among the heavy brigade. The raised running plates over the cylinders, the latter being inclined, gave the engine a lusty appearance that visually seemed to express great power.

Photo: R. Keeley

28. Buxton Road, c.1948. Buxton Road again but, compared to the photograph above, two or three hundred yards nearer to Mersey Square. Car No. 78 is following No. 75 towards Hazel Grove. On the right, beyond and behind the houses is the position of the well known Alma Lodge Hotel. In the distance can be seen the line of shops that were – and still are, a focal point of the Heaviley district. Compare with lower, old postcard view, plate 17.

Photo: F.N.T. Lloyd Jones

29. Buxton Road, c.1910. A pre 1914 view of Buxton Road with the corner of Woodsmoor Lane on the right. Just one tramcar in sight as the two young lads stroll nonchalantly across a road as wide then as now. A few front gardens on the left have gone, otherwise the view in the late 1980s is not greatly changed; that is if one excepts the heavy traffic that now 'graces' the principle main road to the south out of Stockport.

30. Adswood/Davenport, 3rd August 1957. Part of the Buxton line that counts, I think, as one of Stockport's local historic 'ways', and certainly the buildings that frame the picture are of interest. The location is no great distance from the Buxton Road views on this and the following page. The train is the 8.26am Davenport to London Road (before it became Piccadilly). The engine is another Horwich Mogul No. 42858 (a class with a significant history, but I had better not go into that here!). The bridge, known locally as Bakery Bridge, takes Adswood Road over the railway. The Bakery Warehouse, seen on the left, and the chimney formed part of a complex of supply premises for Stockport Co-operative Society.

Photo: Raymond Keeley

31. Wellington Road South, c.1922. A view looking towards Hazel Grove. The corner of Bramhall Lane is somewhat obscured by a large tree and the tram. The card is I think circa the early 1920s and although front gardens are fewer the building line is little changed. The tram, No. 44, is one of the 41–45 series delivered in 1906. They were the first top covered vehicles to operate in the town. Once again, the spire of St Georges Church dominates.

32. Buxton Road, Heaviley. The view on this postcard relates to that depicted on plate 28, but from the other side of the road something like ten years earlier. Some property in the middle distance, left, has been demolished and also the low roofed houses in the left foreground. But otherwise, in respect of the building line, the present day view is easily recognisable.

33. Davenport: Bramhall Lane, c.1910. No tramway! But otherwise a well known 'way' out of Stockport – Bramhall Lane adjacent to Davenport Station. The style of the ancient taxi standing at the station entrance suggests a pre 1914 date for the view. The much narrower cobbled roadway at the junction with Garners Lane makes quite a contrast with the present day scene at this point. Of interest is the station nameboard displaying the company ownership of the time – London and North Western Railway. The stages in road widening over the years show clearly on the underside of the bridge and are easily recognisable these days from the station platform.

34. Wellington Road South. This indeed is a 'meeting of the 'ways''. The point where that 'new road' – Wellington Road South, converges with Hillgate, on the left, to continue south as Buxton Road. Bramhall Lane discreetly passes to the right of the building prominent on the corner that gives cause and effect to a name known locally as 'The Blossoms' – in constant use as a focal point when answering directional enquiries!

35. Mersey Square, c.1948. A rather dramatic view of Manchester bogie car No. 398 heading south out of Mersey Square for Hazel Grove. The unusual lighting in the photograph – it could have been a low but bright late winter sun, seems to underline the almost formidable, but majestic bearing of these superb tramcars.
Photo: J. Fozard

N 4045

Crossley Road	**S.C.T.** Issued subject to the Corporation Bye laws.	Hazelgrove Terminus
Catley Terminus	Available only on Car issued.	Greg Street
Cheadle Church	FARE 4½d	Houldsworth Arms
Farmers' Arms	This Ticket must be shown for inspection when required or given up on demand.	Reddish Terminus
Edgeley Terminus		Pole Bank

Williamson, Printer, Ashton.

36. Mersey Square, c.1947. Looking south up Wellington Road – the photographer is probably standing just in front of the UCP shop – on what appears a rather damp day. The Stockport car has Edgeley as its destination. The Manchester car No. 502 is of the type commonly known as the Pilchers. They were introduced in 1930, the name Pilcher being that of the then new general manager of the system appointed in 1929. The car is, I believe, on a special tour of the Manchester system, which took place on Sunday 30th March 1947 and included the line to Hazel Grove in the itinery. Ian Yearsley's splendid book on the Manchester Tramways gives full details of the Pilchers – an interesting but somewhat controversial design.
Photo: J. Fozard

Up the 'Hill' to Reddish

37. Mersey Square, 15th January 1950. Apart from what appear to be two members of staff, car No. 48 seems to be devoid of passengers. This suggests that it may have just emerged from the depot prior to entering service on the Reddish route, this being the destination showing on the indicator blind.

Part of the entrance to Heaton Lane Depot, built 1924, and its two storey office block and ornamental tower, can be seen on the left.

Photo: J.H. Meredith

Fm0393

Crossley Road	S.C.T.	Belmont Street
Heaton Moor Rd	(issued subject to the Corp'ation Bye-laws. Available only on Car issued.)	St. Peters-gate or Mersey Sq
St. Peters-gate or Mersey Sq		Heaviley Schools
Bramhall Lane		Dialstone Lane
Crown Inn		Hazel Grove Ter
Edgeley Terminus	FARE **1d**	George Hotel
St. Peters-gate		St. Paul Church
Lanca-shire B'ge		Vernon Park
St. Paul's Church	This Ticket must be shown for inspection when required or given up on demand	Travel-ler's Call
Vernon Park		Bredbury Station
Travel-ler's Call		Woodley Station
St. Mark's Church		PoleBank (Woodley)
Williamson		nter, Ashton.

38. Bridge Street, 15th January 1950. An interesting photograph showing the tramway junctions linking Princes Street with Tiviot Dale and Bridge Street. Car No. 55 is about to turn into Tiviot Dale and Lancashire Hill en route to Reddish on a rather damp looking Sunday. Perhaps the ladies in the foreground had been hoping that No. 55 would be on the Vernon Park route! The car seems to merge into a building background from which names appear – among them a well known local tobacconist and optician (see also caption 66).

Photo: J.H. Meredith

LIGHT FIGURES DENOTE A.M. TIMES   DARK FIGURES DENOTE P.M. TIMES

TRAM SERVICES 3, 4a, 35, 35a, 35b, 35c	
3	HAZEL GROVE – REDDISH
4A	HAZEL GROVE – STOCKPORT, St. Peter's Square
35	HAZEL GROVE – STOCKPORT – MANCHESTER, Exchange
35A	STOCKPORT, Mersey Square – MANCHESTER, Exchange
35B	STOCKPORT, St. Peter's Square – MANCHESTER, Albert Square
35C	STOCKPORT, St. Peter's Square – MANCHESTER, Piccadilly

LIGHT FIGURES DENOTE A.M. TIMES   DARK FIGURES DENOTE P.M. TIMES

TRAM SERVICES 3, 35, 35a, 35b, 35c	
3	HAZEL GROVE – REDDISH
35	HAZEL GROVE – STOCKPORT – MANCHESTER, Exchange
35A	STOCKPORT, Mersey Square – MANCHESTER, Exchange
35B	HAZEL GROVE – STOCKPORT – MANCHESTER, Albert Square
35C	STOCKPORT, St. Peter's Square – MANCHESTER, Piccadilly

WEEKDAYS

NOTES : Service Numbers : A—25A. B—35B. C—35C.   R—To Reddish.

SUNDAY

NOTES : Service Numbers : A—35A. B—35B. C—35C.   R—To Reddish.

39. Tiviot Dale, 27th December 1957.
The eastern end of Tiviot Dale station on a rather gloomy day: The train is the 1.30pm Manchester Central to Chinley, hauled by a British Rail Standard Class 4 mixed traffic 2-6-0 No. 76089. Seen in the background are a few of the slender little spires that adorned the Hanover Congregational Chapel, which fronted on to Lancashire Hill. It was built in 1821 and demolished 1966. Further into the background and rather faint, the tower of the magnificent Pendlebury Hall. *Photo: R. Keeley*

Z 7404

OUT	S.C.T.	IN
Heaton Moor Road	Issued subject to the Corporation bye-laws.	Hazelgrove Terminus
Boundary Bridge	Available only on a ...	Houldsworth Arms
Cheadle Heath Station	FARE 4d	Reddish Terminus
Edgeley Terminus	This Ticket must be shown for inspection when required or given up on demand.	Woodley Station
Nelson Hotel		Pole Bank
Williamson	Inter.	Ashton.

40. Tiviot Dale, Lancashire Hill, c.1950. Bottom of the 'Hill'. Car No. 73, on the Reddish to Cheadle Heath service nears the end of the descent of Lancashire Hill. Just in view to the right of the car is part of the Dutch gabled rather ornate frontage of Tiviot Dale Station, demolished in 1968 – a sad loss indeed to Stockport's list of distinguished buildings.

Car No. 73 was one of a batch of ten cars (66–75) ordered in December 1922 to augment the existing fleet, and assist the forthcoming inter-running with Manchester. It was withdrawn in July 1951, just a month before the final abandonment of the system.

Photo: J. Fozard

LIGHT FIGURES DENOTE A.M. TIMES   DARK FIGURES DENOTE P.M. TIMES

TRAM SERVICES 1, 3	1 CHEADLE HEATH—STOCKPORT—REDDISH 3 HAZEL GROVE—STOCKPORT—REDDISH

LIGHT FIGURES DENOTE A.M. TIMES   DARK FIGURES DENOTE P.M. TIMES

TRAM SERVICES 1, 3	1 REDDISH—STOCKPORT—CHEADLE HEATH 3 REDDISH—STOCKPORT—HAZEL GROVE

41. Lancashire Hill, c.1950. Top of the 'Hill'. Car No. 72 has just rounded the corner from Sandy Lane and is commencing the descent of Lancashire Hill. The photograph, though post war, would be pre April 10th 1951, when the Mersey Square–Cheadle Heath section of the Reddish–Cheadle Heath route was withdrawn. Car No. 72 was withdrawn on August 25th 1951 and thus coincided with the final closure of the tram system. *Photo: J. Fozard*

42. Reddish Road, c.1912. An interesting pre 1914 postcard view of Reddish Road looking towards Stockport and taken from just south of the junctions with Vale Road and Greg Street. So what is interesting? Well, the tramlines are there, the trees are there – and doubtless a few of those still survive today; but apart from a very distant tram – one needs a microscope to spot it, not a house or other vehicle in sight.

LIGHT FIGURES DENOTE A.M. TIMES   DARK FIGURES DENOTE P.M. TIMES

TRAM SERVICES 1, 3	1 REDDISH - STOCKPORT - CHEADLE HEATH 3 REDDISH - STOCKPORT - HAZEL GROVE

TRAM SERVICE 3 Bull's Head	REDDISH - STOCKPORT - HAZEL GROVE Rising Sun

Stage No.
1 Reddish, Bull's Head
2 | Longford Road
3 | | Houldsworth Arms
4 1½ | | Vale Road
5 1½ | | | Broadstone Hall Road
6 2 1½ | | | Greg Street
7 2½ 2 1½ | | | Manchester Road
8 3 2½ 2 1½ | | Tiviot Dale
9 3 3 2½ 2 1½ | Mersey Square or St Petersgate
10 3½ 3 2½ 2½ 2 1½ | Longshut Lane
11 4 3½ 3 3 2½ 2 1½ | Bramhall Lane
12 4 4 3½ 3 3 2½ 2 1½ | Heaviley School
13 4½ 4 4 3½ 3 2½ 2 1½ | Kennerley Road
14 4½ 4 4½ 3½ 3 3 2½ 1½ 1½ | Woodsmoor Lane
15 5 4½ 4 4 3½ 3 2½ 2 1½ 1½ | Crown Hotel or Dialstone Lane
16 5½ 5 4½ 4½ 4 3½ 3 2½ 2 1½ 1½ | Commercial Road
17 6 5½ 5 5 4½ 4 4 3½ 2½ 2 1½ 1½ | Hazel Grove, Rising Sun

TRAM SERVICES 4a, 35, 35a, 35b, 35c	4A STOCKPORT, St. Peter's Square—HAZEL GROVE 35 MANCHESTER, Exchange—STOCKPORT—HAZEL GROVE 35A MANCHESTER, Exchange—STOCKPORT, Mersey Square 35B MANCHESTER, Albert Square—STOCKPORT—Hazel Square 35C MANCHESTER, Piccadilly—STOCKPORT, St. Peter's Square

Stage No.
1 Manchester, Albert Square, Exchange, Victoria Street or Piccadilly
2 | Tipping Street or Charles Street
3 1 | Brunswick Street (Ardwick Green) or Ackers Street   ADDITIONAL STAGE
4 1½ | | Plymouth Grove West   Service 35b
5 2 1½ | | Slade Lane, Corner of Stockport Road   Charles Street (Oxford Road) to
6 2½ 2 1½ | | Crowcroft Road or Matthews Lane   Charles Street (Upper Brook Street) 1d.
7 2½ 2½ 2 1½ | | Station Road
6|8 3 3 2½ 2 1½ | | Crossley Road
8 3 3½ 3 2½ 2 1½ | Heaton Moor Road
9 4 4 3½ 3 2½ 2 1½ | Belmont Street
10 4 4½ 4 3½ 3 2½ 2 1½ | Mersey Square or St Petersgate
11 4½ 4½ 4 4 3½ 3 2½ 2 1½ | Longshut Lane
12 5 5 4½ 4 4 3½ 3 2½ 2 1½ | Bramhall Lane
13 5½ 5½ 5 4½ 4 4 3½ 3 2½ 1½ 1½ | Heaviley Schools
14 6 5½ 5½ 5 4½ 4 4 3½ 3 2½ 1½ 1½ | Kennerley Road
15 6 6 5½ 5 4½ 4 4 3½ 3 2½ 2 1½ | Woodsmoor Lane
16 6½ 6½ 6 6 5½ 5 4½ 4 4 3½ 3 2½ 1½ 1½ | Crown Hotel or Dialstone Lane   Commercial Road
17 7 7 6½ 6 6 5½ 5 4½ 4 4 3½ 3 2½ 1½ 1½ | Hazel Grove, Rising Sun

SUNDAY

Reddish, Bull's Head					9 38	9 53	10 8	10 23			12 38	12 53		1 8		1 23	
Houldsworth Square					9 44	9 59	10 14	10 29	Then	12 44	12 59		1 14		1 29		
Greg Street					9 49	10 4	10 19	10 34	every	12 49	1 4		1 19		1 34		
Stockport, Mersey Square	9 09	9 15	9 30	9 45	10 0	10 15	10 30	10 45	15 mins.	1 0	1 12	1 26	1 27	1 36	1 42	1 46	1 56
Cheadle Hth., Boro' Boundary	9 57	2	6 12		26	2 48		until		1 38		1 48		1 58	2	8	
Hazel Grove, Rising Sun	9 22	9 37	9 52	10 7	10 22	10 37	10 52	11 7		1 22	1 34		1 49		2 4		

Reddish, Bull's Head	1 38		1 53		2 8	2 14	10 52				20 26 32 37 44 50 56	2 7 14		5 20 5 26 5 32	
Houldsworth Square	1 44		1 59		2 14	2 20		Then at			26 32 38 43 50 56	2 8 13 20		5 26 5 32 5 38	
Greg Street	1 49		2 4		2 19	2 25		these mins. past each			31 37 43 48 55 1	7 13 18 25		5 31 5 37 5 43	
Stockport, Mersey Square	1 57	2	6 12	18	2 26	2 27	2 36	hour			6 12 16 26 27 36	12 16 27 36	UNTIL	5 41 5 43 5 48 5 56	
Cheadle Hth., Boro' Boundary	2	18		2 28	2 38		2 48				58	8	28 38		48	5 53	6 06	8
Hazel Grove, Rising Sun	2 19		2 34		2 49						4	19	34		49		6 4	

Reddish, Bull's Head	5 37	5 44		5 50	Then every 7½	10 50	10 56		6	7	11	11 16	11 21	11 32	11 37	
Houldsworth Square	5 43	5 50		5 56	mins. to Cheadle	10 56	11	5	6 11	11 16	11 21	11 26	11 32	11 38	11 43	
Greg Street	5 48	5 55		6 1	Heath and every	11 1	11	10	11 16	11 21	11 26	11 31	11 37	11 43	11 48	
Stockport, Mersey Square	5 57	6	3 6 11	6 12	15 mins. to	11 10	11 12	11 18	11 26	11 33	11 40	11 41	11 42	11 48	11 56	11 59
Cheadle Hth., Boro' Boundary					Hazel Grove	11 30										
Hazel Grove, Rising Sun	6 19		6 15	6 23	until		11 34									

Hazel Grove, Rising Sun				9 23		1 23		1 35			10 50	5		5 20	5 35	
Kennerley Road			9 32	Then	1 32		1 44			10 59		11 14		29	44	
Cheadle Hth., Boro' Boundary				every				1 43		11 5		59	5	20	35	
Cheadle Heath Station				15				1 45								
Stockport, Mersey Square	9 11	9 26	9 41	mins.	1 41	1 46	1 53	1 58		3	9 16	24 28	33	39	46	53	5 58
Greg Street	9 19	9 34	9 49	until	1 49	1 54	2	6		11	24 29	37 41	46 52	59	6 11		5 58
Houldsworth Square	9 24	9 39	9 54		1 54	1 59	2	6 21		16	22 29	35 43	47 52	59	6 11		6 4
Reddish, Bull's Head	9 30	9 45	10 0		2	0 2	5 12	12 17		22 28	35 43	47 52 58	5 12 17				6 4

Hazel Grove, Rising Sun		5 35						10 50			11 20		11 33	
Kennerley Road		5 44	Then every 15					10 59		11 14			11 42	
Cheadle Hth., Boro' Boundary	5 40		mins. from				10 55			11 17	11 25		11 29	
Cheadle Heath Station	5 42		Hazel Grove, &				10 57			11 19	11 27		11 34	
Stockport, Mersey Square	5 50	5 53	every 7½ mins.	11 13	11 18			11 24			11 39	11 45	11 51	
Greg Street	6 3	6	from Cheadle	11 13	11 18	11 24								
Houldsworth Square	6 3	6	Heath, until	11 18	11 24		11 29							
Reddish, Bull's Head	6 9	6 12		11 24	11 29	11 35								

Hg2292

S.C.T.

Issued subject to the Corporation Bye-laws. Available only on Car issued.

FARE 2½D

This Ticket must be shown for inspection when required or given up on Band.

Galley to Mersey Square | Mersey Square to Reddish Ter. | Reddish Terminus to Mersey Sq're | Mersey Square to Gat | Woodley Station to Mersey Sq're | Mersey Sq're to Woodley Station

43. Reddish, Broadstone Mill, 6th October 1959. 'The magnificent Broadstone Mill!' – though I am not pretending that the train is incidental. It was probably more by chance that the whole of the mill came into the picture; as I hastily positioned a rather unwieldy bellows camera to 'shoot' a rather interesting train working. It is also a meeting of the 'ways' since the Reddish Canal – which the last carriage of the train has just crossed, followed the line of the mill building. Interesting train working? Yes indeed. It is the 8am ex-Colne, the route being via Burnley, Blackburn, Bolton and Manchester Victoria to Stockport Edgeley, with through carriages for London Euston at Stockport. The engine is Stanier Class 5 No. 44692. *Photo: R. Keeley*

44. Reddish Road, c.1948. Car No. 52 about to top the slight rise which takes Reddish Road across four tracks of railway plus sidings adjacent to Reddish South Station. The station entrance archway and office buildings – demolished in 1968/69 – dominate the right hand side of the photograph. Clearly seen is the change from double to single tram track across the narrow section of road across the bridge.
Photo: F.N.T. Lloyd Jones

45. Reddish Road, n.d. Another interesting view of Reddish Road looking south from the junction of Vale Road and Greg Street. Compared with the view plate 42 this, at least, shows a tramcar en route to Cheadle as a central feature of the picture. Although entitled Willow Grove, that particular location was approximately one mile nearer to Stockport.

46. Reddish, Gorton Road, c.1948. Gorton Road looking north at the junction of Broadstone Road and Houldsworth Square. Car No. 59 travelling to Stockport only. Stone sets, a feature of most late 1940s tram photographs, dominate the foreground of this photograph.   *Photo: F.N.T. Lloyd Jones*

47. Reddish, Gorton Road, c.1948. A few hundred yards further along Gorton Road with Car No. 70 bound for the Bulls Head terminus. At the end of the 1980s, the building line on this and the above photograph is still comfortably familiar. In an ever changing world – and not always for the better, perhaps our emotional feelings require an element of stability; if not only through the presence of familiar shops and buildings that bring a kind of relativity to a district.   *Photo: F.N.T. Lloyd Jones*

48. Reddish, Gorton Road, n.d. A pre-1914 postcard view of Gorton Road, Reddish. The top covered but open balcony and platform tramcar is alongside the Railway Hotel which stands on the north corner of Station Road. Opposite, just beyond the row of shops seen on the right, is the approach to Reddish North Station. How intriguing is the leisurely nonchalant manner of people, when caught by the cameras eye in those early postcard views.

49. Reddish, Gorton Road, c.1948. Something like forty years separates this photograph from the old postcard view above, and for the present day viewer something more like eighty years. And yet, if that early postcard photographer could return – doubtless complete with ancient bellows camera, tripod and glass plates, he would still see little change in the building line!

Photo: F.N.T. Lloyd Jones

50. Reddish, Gorton Road, n.d. This old postcard view perfectly complements the one on the opposite page. The photographer would be standing alongside the Railway Hotel viewing a group of buildings still familiar today. The tramcar destination box, suspended just above where the driver would stand when operating from this end of the vehicle, shows as being en route to Gatley. Familiar in those days, were the grocery and provision shops of T. Seymour Meads. The one on the corner of Station Road being clearly visible.

51. Reddish North Station, 15 June 1957. A midday local train to Hayfield is being hauled by Class C13 4-4-2 tank engine No. 67437. Only part of the original station buildings now survive and they include the rather ornate glass and iron verandah seen on the left of the photograph. You may think the engine is somewhat antique in appearance. Well that is probably because it was built as long ago as 1905, in the Gorton Works of the Great Central Railway. It didn't have long to go after this photograph was taken, its old iron bones being laid to rest just a couple of months later at its place of birth.

So, it outlived all the trams that passed over the bridge in the background. 52 years – not a bad age for a hard working piece of mobile machinery! *Photo: R. Keeley*

| TRAM SERVICE 33 | | | | | MANCHESTER, Victoria St. - REDDISH, Vale Road | | | | |

Stage No.
1						Victoria Street
2	1					Tipping Street
3	1	1				New Manchester Hippodrome
4	1½	1				Clowes Street
5	2	1½	1			Birch Street
6	2½	2	1½	1		Belle Vue, Lake Entrance
7	2½	2	1½	1	1	Wellington Street
8						Chapman Street
9	2½	2½	2	1½	1	L — Reddish Lane Corner
10	2½	2½	2½	2	L — 1 Reddish, Bull's Head
3	3	3	3	2½	2	1 1 Longford Road
3	3½	3½	3½	3	2½	2 — 1½ 1½ 1 Houldsworth Square
4	4	4	4	3½	3	2½ — 2 2 1½ 1 1 Vale Road

AWNINGS
FOR WEDDINGS.
Baize, etc.

MARQUEES
and TENTS for Garden Parties & Fetes

Camping Tents

Tents and Marquees
for Sale or Hire

Stockport Waterproof Factory

ARTHUR LOWE
Manufacturer
22 BROWN ST., STOCKPORT
Phone : STO 2333   Established 1859

LIGHT FIGURES DENOTE A.M. TIMES   DARK FIGURES DENOTE P.M. TIMES

| TRAM SERVICE 33 | | REDDISH, Vale Road—MANCHESTER |

FROM REDDISH

Leave Reddish, Vale Road, for Manchester, Exchange
Monday to Friday at 6.45 a.m. and every 10 minutes until 8.45 a.m., 5.15 p.m. and every 10 minutes until 7.45 p.m.

Saturday at 6.45 a.m. and every 10 minutes until 8.45 a.m., 12.4 p.m. and every 10 minutes until 11.4, 11.24 p.m. Later trams to Devonshire Street only until 12.20 a.m.

Leave Reddish, Vale Road, for Manchester, Piccadilly
Sunday at 9.50, 10.5, 10.20, 10.50 a.m. and every 15 minutes until 10.35 p.m. Later trams to Devonshire Street only until 11.45 p.m.

FROM MANCHESTER

Leave Manchester, Exchange, for Reddish, Vale Road
Monday to Friday at 7.29, 7.39, 7.49, 7.59 a.m., 4.29 p.m. and every 10 minutes until 6.59 p.m.

Saturday at 7.29, 7.39, 7.49, 7.59, 11.29 a.m. and every 10 minutes until 11.39 p.m.

Leave Manchester, Piccadilly, for Reddish, Vale Road
Sunday at 10.15, 10.28 a.m. and every 15 minutes until 1.58, 2.10 p.m. and every 15 minutes until 11.10 p.m.

52. Reddish, c.1949. Passengers dismounting at Reddish terminus. The crossover lines, seen in the foreground, would be used when the car reversed on to the opposite track for the return journey. There was also an overhead trolley reverser – similar to that at Hazel Grove. Car No. 67 belongs to the batch (66–75) built in 1922 to augment the existing fleet in preparation for the forthcoming joint running on the Manchester route. To the left, a Vauxhall encroaches on the scene, the sign beyond – see also picture below – indicating the boundary of the Stockport County Borough.

Photo: J. Fozard

53. (Below) Reddish, c.1949. Reddish terminus again but the reverse of the above view. The tramcar seems to be taking centre stage against an imposing backdrop of buildings that, forty years on, are still familiar to the people of Reddish. The liveliness of the photograph is accentuated by the way the tramlines seem to take a dead set at the viewer. Tramcar No. 56 is one of the 51–60 series, supplied in late 1920–early 1921 and were the first to be in the enclosed form when new. Thornley Lane North is to the left of the picture. Note also the 'intruder' beyond the tram, a Manchester Corporation bus, and square profile of a police telephone box between the road junctions.

Photo: J. Fozard

54. Reddish Bridge, c.1922. Strictly speaking this, and the photograph below, are beyond the normal working area of Stockport trams, however I felt that they must be included, especially as both show different views of what might be termed a focal point of North Reddish, that of Reddish Bridge, a familiar landmark to the local people and those from surrounding districts, particularly in the days when the canal was in operation. The Manchester tram, No. 404, is en route to Denton. The route number 57 would, at the time the photograph was taken, indicate an Ashton–Denton working. Quite possibly, 404 would be working on to that route later. The style of dress suggests an early 1920s photograph and how superbly the picture captures the easy nonchalant way passengers could stroll into the middle of the road in those days.

Photo: E. Gray

55. Reddish Bridge, c.1946. A rather dramatic view of two Manchester trams at the junction of Reddish Lane and Hyde Road, the handsome lines of 949 – en route to Vale Road, showing to great advantage. The photograph is, I believe, early post war, since the service to Vale Road* from Manchester ceased operation on February 1st 1948. The car in the background, coming from the Denton direction, is one of the 'Pilchers' introduced in 1930.

* Rush hours only

Photo: J. Fozard

56. Reddish, 22nd July 1948.
Judging by this, and photographs 63 and 67, it really was a wet day in Stockport. However, the damp glitter does convey something of the atmosphere all too often associated with our part of the world. It is interesting to compare this photograph of car No. 34 with that of car No. 33 in the old postcard view at Hazel Grove (plate 21). Perhaps its the dank appearance of the day that gives No. 34 a slightly weary look. However, forty three years hard work must make any vehicle of the road look its age – whatever the weather! The top covers on the 31–40 series of cars were fitted during 1907–8, and the platforms vestibuled 1937–38.

Photo: R.J.S. Wiseman

57. Reddish, c.1948. Car No. 53 has moved over the crossover that can be seen in both photographs 52 and 53 and it is now framed by a group of buildings still familiar in the late 1980s. A nine or ten year old, like the young lady standing outside Coffeys, would now, forty years on, be approaching... Well, time does march on, certainly for humans if not necessarily for buildings!

Photo: J. Fozard

58. Reddish, n.d. This picture postcard will be, I think, self explanatory for Reddish residents, both past and present. It is postmarked 29th November 1918 – ten days after the Armistice. The message, from a lady named Annie to her friend Florrie, and infers a safe return from the wars of at least one man. Interesting, that even on a postcard the viaduct was referred to as The Arches, in my youth it was the '16 arches'!

59. Reddish, 11th August 1958. I have included this railway photograph because, once again, the location will be familiar to residents of Reddish. I was standing by one of a small number of railway public footpath crossings in the Stockport area. It connected a field path to another field path in those days, just west of Windmill Lane and it is of course still in use. The train is the 5.49 Manchester London Road to Macclesfield. The presence of this type of engine is interesting, because nominally, a JII class 64341 would be more used to hauling goods trains at a sedate pace. On occasion however, it was possible to see regular workings by locomotives not even considered to be what were called mixed traffic engines; and, at that time, 64341 would be getting on in years, having been built in 1904 for the Great Central Railway at that other place only a short distance away, Beyer Peacock & Co.

Photo: R. Keeley

60. Reddish, CWS Printing Works, c.1964. This photograph is probably unique, since my viewing point would not normally be available to the general public. The Broadstone Mill as seen from the top of the fire escape steps at the rear of the C.W.S. Printing Works – my place of work for over thirty years. Just visible in the foreground is a rather overgrown section of the Stockport Branch of the Ashton Canal. The goods train is on the line that passes through Reddish South Station. A once very important line (and should still be) that saw heavy goods traffic in those days. The main reason for including the photograph is that it shows the beginning of the demolition of the mill chimneys. The top section of the near chimney has already gone, gradually reduced brick by brick. Unfortunately I did not record the date, which was unusual and quite remiss of me, although I believe it was in the late summer of 1964 when demolition of some of the buildings began.

Photo: R. Keeley

61. (Right) Reddish Road. Car No. 24 approaching the top of the railway bridge adjacent to Reddish South Station at a point where the double track reduced to single across the bridge, returning to a double formation on the opposite side. The destination indicator suggests the car is on a short working to Houldsworth Square, where it will reverse for the return to Stockport and thence Dialstone Lane on the Hazel Grove route. The double H.H. on the same circular front panelling – known as the Dash, indicates it to be a low bridge car suitable to work under the two low bridges on the Hyde route. No. 24 was one of the ten original batch of cars to retain the right hand ascending – or reverse, spiral staircase, clearly seen in the photograph. *Photo: F.E.J. Ward*

Ac 8952

Crossley Road	S.C.T.	Dialstone Lane
Belmont Street	Issued subject to the Corp'ation Bye-laws.	Hazel Grove Ter
Catley Terminus	Available only on Car issued.	Tiviot Dale
Cheadle Church	FARE	Greg Street
Farmers' Arms	3½d	Houldsworth Arms
Nelson Hotel	This Ticket must be shown for inspection when required or given up as demanded.	Woodley Station
St. Petersgate		Woodley (Pole Bank)

Williamson, Printer, Ashton.

Ct 5924

Crossley Road	S.C.T.	Mersey Sq or St. Petersgate
Belmont Street	Issued subject to the Corp'ation Bye-laws.	Heaviley Schools
Mersey Square or St. Petersgate	Available only on Car issued.	Woodsmoor Lane
Longshut Lane		Dialstone Lane
Kennerly Road		Hazel Grove Far
Edgeley Terminus	FARE	Lancashire B'ge
Nelson Hotel	1½d	Pear Mill
Travel-ler's Call		Pole Bank
Cheadle Church	This Ticket must be shown for inspection when required or given upon demand.	Cheadle Heath 3'n
Farmers' Arms		Tiviot Dale
M'chester Old Road		Houldsworth Arms
Vale Road		Reddish Terminus

Williamson, Printer, Ashton.

62. (Below) Reddish Road, c.1948. A view clearly showing the road alignment on the approach to the railway bridge at South Reddish Station. Greg Street is on the left, Vale Road on the right. Part of the intricate arrangement for holding the overhead wiring in position at a wide road junction can also be seen in this photograph. It is perhaps difficult to visualise nowadays the crowds that were likely to disgorge from the trams for the short walk to Cravens, now merely a name in the list of notable Stockport engineering firms that have vanished in more recent times. *Photo: F.N.T. Lloyd Jones*

63. Reddish Road, 22nd July 1948. Relative to the previous photograph since car No. 57 is standing at the stop which can be seen in that picture. The junction with Vale Road is on the opposite side of the main road, just behind the queue of people waiting to board an already well filled tram. An obviously damp gloomy day with rain macs very much in evidence, almost contradicting the summer date – but such is our climate! *Photo: R.J.S. Wiseman*

64. Lancashire Hill, n.d. Top of the 'Hill' again – compare with caption for plate 41. Car No. 62 is heading towards Stockport – though the destination blind shows Vale Road! An oversight one assumes; the sort of occasional slip that happens in the best regulated tram, bus and even railway organisations! *Photo: R.J.S. Wiseman*

65. (Right) Tiviot Dale, 5th April 1957. Another glance in passing at Tiviot Dale Station. I had been passenger on the train, the 1.04 pm Manchester Central–Chinley, from which I made a rapid exit. Dashing over the footbridge, running along the opposite platform and at the same time feverishly adjusting my somewhat unwieldy bellows camera. It was worth it as I was just in time to get one of my favourite photographs of a 'Compound' in action. The 'Midland Compounds' – the elite of Midland Railway express engines, were, in my opinion, among the most beautiful and graceful locomotives ever built. No. 41118 was recently ex works and quite resplendent (I had also taken one or two photographs of her at Central before we departed). It was probably her last major overhaul, since old age now had her in its grip. The engine was built in 1925 (in LMS days, but that is another story) and withdrawn January 1958. Though not pin sharp, the photo has caught the wheel slip and the angry bellow as the engine restarts on the climb towards Romiley. A demonstration indeed of the fiery interior that lay beneath an elegant exterior.

Photo: Raymond Keeley

66. (Below) Tiviot Dale, c.1950. Bottom of the 'Hill' again. Car No. 56 rounds the tightest curve on the system, (other than in the two depots) from Tiviot Dale into Princes Street, with a radius of 33 feet. The shops and buildings in the background are, to say the least, interesting, still there but of different uses.

Photo: R.W.A. Jones

67. Princes Street, 22nd July 1948. A rather damp murky day, but what an interesting photograph. The Tiviot Dale end of Princes Street and, I feel, an unusual tram photographic point as Car No. 38 awaits while Car No. 5 clears the single line section, seen between the two cars. The sign on the right draws attention – discreetly, to the presence of Ellis Sykes show rooms, a site now occupied by Toy and Hobby.

Photo: R.J.S. Wiseman

GARNER & SON

ARTHUR GARNER, F.A.I.   A. GARNER, Junr., F.S.I.

HOUSE AND LAND AGENTS

VALUERS AND SURVEYORS

Prudential Buildings	Northern Assurance Bldgs.
St. Petersgate	Albert Square
STOCKPORT	**MANCHESTER**
Telephone—STO 3013-4	Telephone—BLA 5291

68. Princes Street, 1951. The interesting building lines of Princes Street frame Car No. 56 which appears to be proceeding towards Mersey Square; although it is more likely that the photograph was taken in the last few months of the tram system when – after the closure of Cheadle Heath service on April 10th 1951, the loop on Princes Street was used as a terminal point for the Reddish service. Indeed, I would have thought that were it otherwise, the gentleman, with confident stride, who is about to cross the tracks, might be in danger of being knocked down! The passing loop, on what had been a busy section of single track, can just be seen to the rear of the tram.

Photo: J. Fozard

69. Wellington Road N/Princes Street, 14th May 1949. A photograph taken on May 14th 1949 with an unidentified car turning into Princes Street; it would of course be operating on either the Reddish or Vernon Park route. With a motor car appearing on the left and buses front and rear of the tram – birds of ill omen so to speak, the photograph seems, unconsciously, to portray a pictorial version of 'the writing on the wall', for indeed the death knell had long been sounding its mournful lament for a tramway system conceived with such high hopes half a century earlier. The Touchstone Inn protrudes on the left.

Photo: A.D. Packer

70. Princes Street/Mersey Square, 23rd February 1950. Car about to turn out of Princes Street bound for Edgeley; the route being Wellington Road South, Greek Street and Castle Street, terminating at Dale Street, a run which was part of route No. 2 Edgeley–Hyde. After closure of the through route to Hyde on March 2nd 1947 – due to a decision by S.H.M.D. joint board to abandon the tramway from Pole Bank to Hyde, the service was reduced to Vernon Park–Edgeley service although some peak hour journeys to Woodley continued until May 3rd 1947. *Photo: R.B. Parr, National Transport Museum*

Short run to Edgeley

71. Wellington Road South, 15th January 1950. There is, for me, a sense of real movement in this January 15th 1950 photograph. Car No. 12 hurrying away from the 'Square' en route to Edgeley. It seems almost to be pacing that other familiar vehicle of the roads in those early post war days, the motor bike and sidecar. Cars between Hyde and Edgeley commenced using the new, up line, over Wellington Bridge – instead of travelling via Daw Bank and St Petersgate, from January 1924.

Photo: J.H. Meredith

72. Mersey Square. An interesting old postcard view showing a car on the original route to Edgeley via St Peters Square and St Petersgate, the return being down Wellington Road South and the single track over Wellington Bridge to Mersey Square. A destination board, showing Edgeley–Hyde, can be seen across the middle window of the saloon. The scene shows to advantage the distinctive building and tower of Stockport Fire Station. Missing of course, is the ornate frontage of the tram depot, which was not built until 1929.

FIRE STATION, STOCKPORT

326.

73. Wellington Road South, c.1907. A view from an old postcard looking south from the corner of St Petersgate, the postmark on the back being November 1907. The building to the left foreground is the Mechanics Institute, built 1862 and demolished 1912. It was replaced by Stockports Central Library building, opened in 1913. The remaining building line on the left is still recognisable today, although the large building next to the Town Hall, known as Ebenezer Chapel, has been demolished. The approach to Edgeley Station can be seen on the right. In those days the word London – easily discernable, would refer to London and North Western Railway. Of particular interest are the tramlines in the foreground, showing tracks curving north and south out of St Petersgate. That in the immediate foreground will join the single track, seen on the right, running back to Mersey Square. At that time it was used by Manchester cars on their circular pattern route from Mersey Square via St Peters Square and St Petersgate back to Mersey Square. The single track from St Petersgate and down Wellington Road South to Mersey Square was not doubled, by the addition of an up line, until 1923. The track curving south towards the tramcar becomes, in effect, the up section of track towards Hazel Grove. The tram seen in the background, is turning into Wellington Street and will then traverse Lord Street into St Peters Square.

74. Wellington Road South, c.1910. The reverse of the view seen above and probably of a slightly later date. Part of the roof line of the Mechanics Institute can just about be seen to the left of the distant tramcar. Ebenezer Chapel is more clearly seen in this view, next to the Town Hall. The foundation stone for the Town Hall was laid on October 15th 1904 and officially opened by the Prince and Princess of Wales on July 7th 1908.

In the foreground can be seen the tramlines, and even more prominently the overhead wires, curving towards Greek Street and the Edgeley route.

75. Shaw Heath, c.1905. A view of the Armoury Square taken from Shaw Heath, on an old, Edwardian period, postcard. The Armoury Tower still dominates the area and is quite a local landmark. Other buildings on the right also remain and are, the Armoury Inn, District Bank (now Nat West) and a corner of the Swan Inn. The tramcar emerging on the left from Castle Street is probably one of the 31–40 series of cars built initially for the electrification of the Edgeley and Hazel Grove routes in 1905. They were the first series to be built with the left hand turning spiral staircase. Originally open top (see also plate 22) they received top covers in 1907–8. Horse trams had previously operated both routes. On 13th April 1905, track reconstruction and the provision of above ground structures and wiring for the intricate work of electrification commenced. Both lines were reopened to the public on 5th July 1905. One wonders if, eighty odd years later, such a relatively involved and large scale operation would have been completed so quickly? During the period of reconstruction a service was provided by horse buses.

76. Stockport Edgeley, 1st June 1959. This photograph shows part of the northern end of the railway tunnel beneath Armoury Square; albeit some years beyond the age of the tram. The train emerging from the tunnel was due into Edgeley at 5.57 pm and conveyed through carriages from Swansea. Obviously it must have been a minute or two late since I had just photographed the train moving out on the left – the 5.58 Comet to London Euston, so I needed to do a quick about turn. 45554 is a Jubilee Class 4-6-0 name *Ontario*, and, in my opinion, one of W.A. Staniers most elegant designs.
Photo: R. Keeley

77. Castle Street, 7th January 1950. Short run to Edgeley it may have been, but it provided a means of public transport for a thriving compact community which, in the first decade of the century, would, from around its southern edge, have a view over farmland and fairly open country. The original intention had been to continue the route along Edgeley Road and make contact with the Gatley route on Stockport Road Cheadle Heath. In fact a complex triangular junction was actually constructed adjacent to the Farmers Arms, but the plan never came to fruition, the junction being removed in 1910. The Saturday afternoon importance of the route also became apparent when Stockport County were playing at home. Then the western end of Castle Street would see a line up of special cars, as in the above photograph.
Photo: D.F. Tee

78. Dale Street, c.1949. Car No. 23 is seen here at the Dale Street terminus in the late 1940s, the destination indicator clearly showing a return to Vernon Park. An interesting visual feature of Stockport cars was the variation in shape of the curved enclosed end sections. A noticeable flattening of the central section of the curve was associated with later series of cars – perhaps being most obvious in the shape of the Dash. The 51–60 series wee the first batch with this feature. Earlier cars, with a few exceptions, retained a more completely rounded end section. *Photo: A.D. Packer*

79. Castle Street, c.1949. Car No. 6 heading back towards the distant Castle Street shops. Some property on the left of the photograph was eventually demolished to make way for the construction of Mercian Way.

Photo: F.E.J. Ward

Westward to Gatley

The first few photographs illustrating this section are a group of contrasting views showing how the Gatley–Reddish route made its sinuous entrance and exit from Mersey Square before sweeping away westward under Wellington Road South. Cars from Reddish, emerging from Princes Street, followed a series of reverse curves that formed, in effect, the slightly angular shape of an S before they faced west once again.

80. Mersey Square, c.1948. Passengers board Car No. 70 from the tram shelter that stood approximately in the middle section of the S bend. The graceful lines of the tramcar are partially framed by the ornate and decorative frontage of the Stockport Fire Station, built in 1902. It was a fine building that made a contribution to the character of Mersey Square and a legacy, now discarded, from a distinguished age of architectural beauty which we are now, perhaps, beginning to appreciate.

Photo: J. Fozard

81. (Below) Mersey Square. This old postcard view relates to the one in plate 19 and also dates from pre-1914. The car rounding the bend is, I believe No. 37 (the 31–40 series of cars received their top covers during 1907–8. See also Plate 5). The destination box – suspended from the canopy circle just above the drivers head, proclaims that it is en route to Gatley. To the right of the picture, a four wheeled open top Manchester car is about to proceed up Daw Bank to St Peters Square. Daw Bank at this point has, at different times, been known as Rock Row, St Peters Square, and Mersey Square.

82. Mersey Square, 21st February 1950. A quite dramatic photograph, with the distinctive profile of the Mersey Hotel towering in the background, as car No. 72 waits to proceed towards the interlaced double track section beneath the arch under Wellington Road South. *Photo: I.A. Yearsley*

83. Mersey Square, c.1936. An opposite and rather earlier view, compared to that above. This time the car seems to be on the move towards the interlaced track. The New Mersey Bridge, mentioned on the postcard, is, in effect, the first stage in the building of Merseyway. The new bridge, completed during the years 1934–5, required the re-modelling of the old bridge and considerable widening of the adjacent area towards the Wellington Road Arches.

84. Chestergate, c.1950. Car No. 56 operating on the Reddish–Cheadle Heath service; the lines to Cheadle Heath not being finally abandoned until 10th April 1951. No. 56 is from the 51–60 series of cars, built for the Corporation in 1920/21. All survived until the end of the tram system. The interlacing of the tracks beneath the arch allowed cars to pass under at the highest point and still leave room for the overhead power wiring. The arch that the tram has passed under is today used as an exit way for buses leaving the bus station, while the arch to the right usually sees would-be passengers scurrying into the bus station.

Photo: J. Fozard

85. Chestergate, c.1950. Just a few yards further on than the view above, but what a difference that short distance makes to the vista, so much more now included. In particular the fact that it shows two cars at right angles – and one travelling above the other! The upper one of course is on Wellington Road South. I am not aware of a similar situation elsewhere on British tramways. The bridge across the river can be seen to the left, also the iron railings which are still in situ. Factory buildings replaced by bus shelters make for a dramatic change of scene.

Photo: F.N.T. Lloyd Jones

86. Cheadle Heath: Stockport Road, c.1910. August 1911 is the postmark on the reverse of this view taken from an old postcard, plus a touchingly simple message from a lady named Edi to her friend Maggie. The tram, on Stockport Road Cheadle Heath, is approaching the bridge over the railway and is en route to Gatley – the letters can just about be seen on the destination indicator.

87. Cheadle Heath Station, 3rd April 1959. The 7.30am Manchester Central–Derby approaching Cheadle Heath Station on the 3rd April 1959. The modest four coach train will be no problem for the powerful locomotive No. 73157 a Class 5 mixed traffic design built by British Railways. The train, after passing through Heaton Mersey Station, will have crossed the high level viaduct seen in plate 3. To the left can be seen the last couple of Hoppers and brake van of a limestone empties train returning to Peak Forest. The lines to the left passed under Stockport Road bridge and curved away to Cheadle Junction.

88. Cheadle Heath Station, 12th April 1958. The carriage sidings at Cheadle Heath. The former Midland Railway type 0-6-0s, 43243 and 43715, are backing towards the station to take out a southbound goods train. The Fowler 2-6-2 tank No. 40001 will later move into the station to take out a local train to Manchester Central. Seen to the right are two ancient Midland Railway Pullman type carriages, now minus bogies, they provided staff accommodation. The sidings are now replaced by housing adjacent to Bird Hall Lane.

89. Cheadle Heath Station, 12th April 1958. Another glance at Cheadle Heath Station on the 12th April 1958. Jubilee Class 4-6-0 45557 *New Brunswick*, hurries the 7.25am Manchester Central–St Pancras on the long upward grind towards Peak Forest. The goods yards on the left are now occupied by various business premises. Perhaps, with a little more foresight twenty years ago, Cheadle Heath, with ample space for 'park and ride', could have been a really useful out of town terminus for a light rail system. I see it as just one more lost opportunity, among those we are still in process of losing!   *Photos: R. Keeley*

90. Cheadle Heath: Boundary Bridge, 15th February 1950. The tramways in the Urban District area of Cheadle and Gatley were finally replaced by buses in 1931. This, it would seem, was the result of some disagreement between the Urban District Council and Stockport Tramways Committee concerning the partial replacement of the tramway system by buses and problems of parity in the relative fare structures, etc. Thus, Boundary Bridge Cheadle Heath, became the terminus for the service from Reddish during the last twenty years of tramway operation At Cheadle Heath terminus, car No. 38 uses the crossover between the tracks in preparation for the return journey to Mersey Square and Reddish. Meanwhile, car No. 9 awaits to make the same manoeuvre. The drivers appear to be having a few brief words – in passing; so to speak. *Photo: D.F. Tee*

91. Cheadle Heath: Stockport Road/Kenilworth Road, 15th February 1950. Since there are, for a number of reasons, a comparative abundance of tram photographs covering the few years between the mid 1940s and the end of the system, it follows that Cheadle Heath saw far more camera activity than those places, farther to the west, where the system had been long abandoned. It would seem that car No. 5 caught a glimpse of westerly sun at Cheadle Heath as it stands ready and waiting to commence a return journey. Destination Reddish, on 15th February 1950, can clearly be seen on the indicator. *Photo: D.F. Tee*

92. Stockport Road, Cheadle, c.1948.
Cheadle Heath terminus again, with car No. 75 waiting to return to Reddish. Driver and conductor are easing their legs with a well earned few minutes of repose, just inside the lower saloon.

Photo: F.E.J. Ward

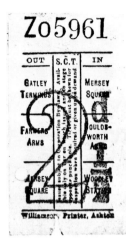

93. Cheadle, The White Hart, c.1904.
More a view of the tram-way than the vehicle itself, which just manages to squeeze in on the left. Something of a focal point in the village, the notice boards no doubt contain details of many of the attractions available by rail excursion, well supported by the masses for whom personal transport was not even a dream.

94. Gatley Road, Cheadle, c.1910.
This old postcard view is, I would think, quite rare. It shows a tram en route from Gatley to Reddish – the destination is just about readable. The car, No. 30 – with the right hand ascending staircase clearly visible, is approaching the bend that will lead it into Cheadle High Street. The houses in the background are on Milton Crescent.

Three interesting photographs of trams at Gatley (Horse and Farrier) terminus, in the early days of the system, all reproduced by permission of Stockport M. B. Libraries

95. Car No. 33 – I think. This series received their top covers in 1907–8 and I would say that the photograph dates from about that time. The wooden framed removable destination indicators can be seen in the middle window of the saloon. The lettering was printed on celluloid and, after dark, could be read against the lighting from inside the car. It reads, Gatley–Cheadle–Stockport–Reddish.

Fr 1662

Crossley Road	S.C.T.	Heaviley Schools
Heaton Moor Rd	Issued subject to the Corporation Bye-laws.	Woods-moor Lne
Belmont Street		Dialstone Lane
Longshut Lane	Available only on Car issued.	Hazel Grove Ter
Gatley Terminus	FARE	Cheadle He'th Stn
Cheadle Church	2½d	Tiviot Dale
Farmers Arms		Greg Street
Manches Ter Road	This Ticket must be shown for inspection	Reddish Terminus
Nelson Hotel		Bradbury Station
St. Paul Church		Fole Bank
William , Printer, Ashton,		

96. Car No. 22 ready for the return journey. Prominently displayed is the metal box destination indicator fitted at each end of the car above the top guard rail. Also the brackets, originally fitted on the rail above the ventilator lights, into which route boards could be slotted.

97. Car No. 23, plus staff and passengers, pose for the photographer. The right hand ascending spiral staircase, originally fitted to the first thirty cars (and retained by ten of them) shows very clearly. It was supposed to give drivers some protection from the rain. Could there also have been a head bumping potential and restriction of view problem that influenced the decision to standardise on the left hand ascending type of stairway?

Youthful Impressions and Memories

Arguably, the heyday of the tramcar in Britain could be said to have occurred between the close of one great war in 1918 and the beginning of a second in 1939. Arguably? Well yes, at least from my point of view, because the images, the impressions, that make an indelible mark on our lives, depend on age. Consider the wonder of childhood, seeing the world with eyes uncluttered with the sadness and cynicism of life's experience. A happy childhood can be remembered in adulthood when the innocent wonder can no longer be reproduced.

My childhood and early teen years coincided with the period mentioned and, for a young lad fascinated from an early age by all forms of transport on road, railway, and the sea, it was a marvellous time. In those days the traffic, even on the main roads, was comparatively sparse, especially when compared to the present day undignified clutter that, with nerve jangling haste or frustrated congestion, creates, for drivers and pedestrians alike, its own vision of bedlam.

The road traffic of the 1920s and early 30s, being generally more intermittent and travelling at a leisurely pace, brought a kind of dignity to what might describe as – a rate of vehicular movement more akin to what had been the pulse of human life for many centuries. At that time a still considerable horse drawn traffic would only slowly become reduced as it succumbed to a still primitive form of motorised transport. But, as the great cart horses nodded between the shafts of four wheeled wagons, bringing, as it seemed, a benign form of movement to the city streets and helping retain something of the sanity of nature, one could have wished for time to stand still.

Whatever their toil these 'best friends of man' presented a majesty of bearing beyond compare. Clatter they did, and sometimes slide – across the cobbles, but dignity remained intact as they struggled and tugged, with manifest strain, between the shafts of piled high drays or a van. The iron bound wooden wheels sometimes protested a little as they swivelled diagonally across the tramlines at a right turn, and occasionally produced a spark as metal ground against stone sett, the hind legs of the beast of burden straining and stretching back with the extra effort needed to quickly turn the corner.

A more slimly built product of the same species would skip lightly between the shafts of less ponderous vehicles, which came in a variety of types. It could be an open cart on two wheels, each covered by a shapely mudguard, carrying – precariously balanced as it seemed to me, several churns of white slopping liquid from the local dairy. Or, alternatively, a small van – that could be described as a near relation to the Hansom Cab, an elegant vehicle on two wheels and again, with a pair of shapely mudguards. As a child I associated it with a delicious aroma, its interior infused with the fresh and appetising smell of the products of the local bakery and ready to deliver to the housewifes door or the local shop.

The main road scene of those days would also, on occasion, be enhanced and enlivened by the presence of that comparitively short lived phenomenon. the steam lorry. A hybrid product of that brief period of experiment, when steam tangled between horse power and petrol. Sadly, it was an anachronism – at least as a road lorry, almost before it was born. This gorgeously pompous but fascinating machine would hiss and puff along with its load of bricks, barrels or whatever, the driver twirling a hand wheel attached to a lengthy steering rod which, through cogs and bevelled wheels, operated chains that tugged left or right to swivel the front wheels, the solid rubber tyres around thick spoked wheels giving a leaden footed impulse to their slow rate of progress.

98. Stockport Road, Levenshulme, c.1908. An old postcard postmarked 1909, a view prominently displaying the one time Urban District Offices – or Levenshulme Town Hall as it was known. The U.D.C. was incorporated into Manchester in 1909, and this fine building of 1898 now finds a different use. The remaining building line has changed very little during the intervening 80 years.

The trams that feature on this, and the old postcard views on the following three pages, are all Manchester cars; which were responsible for operating the Stockport–Manchester routes in the first 21 years of operation.

In my imagination, these machines displayed temperament, spirit, and a kind of benevolent humanity. Characters they indeed were and quite the equal, in my youthful opinion, to the ex-Great Central Railway passenger engines with their fascinating names, the same that thundered along that section of one time main line between Levenshulme South Station and Hyde Road, with their long rakes of elegant carriages. Who, I wondered, in my innocence, was *Sir Sam Fay*? or *Butler Henderson* – an intriguing name to say the least. But *Valour*, *Zeebrugge*, *Somme* – well, 1914–18 was recent enough, and various uncles had talked sufficiently about that war to give me a few ideas.

Steam wagons, steam locomotives, both amply possessed of character, but how they differed. If the steam wagon conjures up a picture of the honest toiling labourer, trousers stringed round the knees, clay pipe at a jaunty angle, then the gleaming express engine becomes a legendary knight in shining armour, taking flight to break the fetters that keep it earthbound. The heroic pace, and the extrovert displays of power; unleashed as they charged under a favourite little footbridge near Broom Lane, held me spellbound. Taking flight! Well, I little knew then that the thunder of their passage towards Woodhead was the result of gravity taking its toil – and earthbound they would remain!

The motor car blossomed from the classics of Edwardian design into the elegant shapes of the 1920s and early 30s, adding to the rich variety of wheeled traffic seen at that time on the roads, but – whether horse drawn, petrol or steam driven, each had, perchance, to bow to a supremo of the highway – the tramcar! Its like had never been seen before and, with its combination of grace, power and 'presence', will probably never be seen again – well not in such a compelling profile!

When compared to the tramcar – especially as it reached towards a zenith of its development in the form of the enclosed double decked vehicle, all other traffic seemed to assume a kind of coughing jogging nature, which then tended to emphasise the gliding bustling importance of this unchallenged monarch of all it surveyed.

Though the final development of the tramcar body in the first half of this century gradually progressed towards an almost totally enclosed form, I always favoured, as a boy, the cars with the 'open to the elements' driving platform and the equivalent open balcony on the top deck. Though I cannot possibly imagine that the drivers of such vehicles who, in winter – and more than just occasionally in summer – had to put brave face to whatever the elements had to offer, would have agreed. The roof over his head gave but little protection, since the weather – wet or dry – would, through the cars movement, tend to drive horizontally at him.

Just think of him standing at the controls, yes – standing! Peering along darkened roads, with the constant need to remain alert while both hands manipulated the controls; and with the attendant leg aching job of keeping on your feet on a swaying vehicle during a several hours stint. An exhausting job indeed especially at times when you were feeling a bit unwell, but such were the hazards of the drivers life during much of the tramway period.

Imagine what it would be like in the gloom of mid winter days, with the stinging lash of rain or snow as it swept into the front of the car; or the bone chilling bitterness of an east wind when travelling up to Gee Cross. Albeit he would be wearing a heavy overcoat plus scarf and gauntlet gloves, but when the temperature came near to zero, a cold wet shivering body was likely to be a condition that had to be endured, especially as many of the earlier

99. Stockport Road, Levenshulme, c.1906. The junction of Stockport Road and Albert Road at what was know as Levenshulme Tram Terminus; it being a terminus for certain short route workings. The loop line adjacent to the main double tracks could be used by cars waiting to make a return working. The destination indicator of the car on the left shows Exchange (Manchester), the one on the right shows Stockport. The building line on each side has not, to this day, greatly changed although the 'new' Pack Horse Hotel, built in the late Edwardian period, now replaces the old building on the far right of the picture. The card is postmarked 1907.

cars retained their open platform for a lengthy period of their lives.

However, such hazards were not likely to worry the young lad hastening up the curving twisting iron stairway, holding tight to the metal handrails, for the stairway ends seemed to catch and emphasise each jerk and jolt. A scramble between the clattering wooden seats (the back rests being reversible to accord with the direction of travel) of the upper saloon, then through the sliding doorway onto the front 'outside' balcony. Here, the spartan slatted wooden seats, curved to fit the end shape of the car, might be a little rain wetted – not that youthful enthusiasm was ever deterred (unless mum insisted that we should sit 'inside') the birds eye view through the guard rails making it all worthwhile.

Gazing down at the lesser fry of the road, the cars, lorries etc, veering away from the tramtracks when the driver stamped urgently on the alarm bell at his feet, one felt involved in the commanding manner exerted by this irresistable vehicle. From that vantage point the approach to a junction of lines or a crossing could easily be observed and thus the agitated complaint from the car, as it crossed, could be anticipated.

Since I lived in the Levenshulme district in the early 1920s and early 1930s, many of my tram journeys commenced on Stockport Road. If the ride was towards Manchester the excitement would quickly increase for, within minutes, the tram would pass under the railway bridge and approach the junction at Slade Lane. A moment of apprehension would follow, then the lurch and grind as we crossed the points, the sensation being both felt and audible. Then, within a couple of hundred yards of so, we would arrive at the formidable right angle crossing and junction at Dickenson Road/Stanley Grove. At this point the enchanting single deck cars on Manchester's 53 route crossed Stockport Road – much loved

and used – especially when we were going 'to see Auntie Lizzie at Cheetham Hill'! At the crossing, the double bogies of the Manchester cars made a great furore, the seats seeming to flutter and vibrate, every panel and pinion appearing to be on the move, bare knees and legs feeling every bit via the lattice work of the seats!

For the observer standing on the pavement at this spot the formidable Manchester Trams made an impressive sight. The ornate livery, bright red and ivory coloured, superbly embellished with golden brown lining and coloured glass half lights – elegance personified! Then, a slow motion charge as two sets of four wheeled bogies hiccuped precariously – or so it seemed, across the right gaps in the rails.

The Stockport cars, also a familiar sight on Stockport Road during my early and then teenage years of tram riding, both into Stockport and Manchester, were rather smaller than a big Manchester bogie cars. With the body of the car overhanging at each end of the fixed four wheel truck, it could be said, that in their style of movement, they nodded and swayed a little. This very gentle 'life on the ocean wave' sensation, did however make for a rather easier ride – if that was what you wanted, especially when points and crossings had to be negotiated. A choice between a rather more rhythmic motion as compared to the rumble and thunder of the Manchester cars.

When I consider the above, rather personal impressions, it would almost seem that I am describing two different species – a kind of male/female connotation! My imagination taking flight you might think – well maybe. And yet, as I saw it at the time, the Stockport cars were not only smaller, they also appeared more dainty. An attribute accentuated by the elegant way they travelled along the rails. They seemed to display a grace of movement rare in what was

100. Stockport Road/Slade Lane, Longsight, c.1907. This old postcard view – though not very clear, just had to be used in the book. It shows the junction of Slade Lane and Stockport Road. The old toll house – at what my mother always referred to as 'the corner of Slade Lane', is remembered by me in very early childhood as a shop that sold toffees and toys. An interesting variant of the horse drawn cart is the hand cart on the left being hauled by human power. The card is postmarked April 1908.

still a comparitively large vehicle of the road. Thus came the impression that they were just lightly touched with a kind of feminine magic, compared to which, the Manchester cars appearing massive and powerful of limb, suggested more of the muscular thrust associated with the male of the species. Indeed one could see them as Manchesters own fiery chariots, dominant and indomitable.

Though Stockport didn't, so far as I am aware, aspire to the large double bogie style of car that gradually found favour on some other systems, they did go through the development pangs experienced by other companies. Open tops, open balconies and platforms in the beginning before proceeding through a gradual sequence towards a more enclosed type of vehicle. Wooden seating initially, although this graduated to comfortable leather upholstered seating in later years, both upstairs and down on some of the cars. A form of moquette upholstery could also be enjoyed in some lower saloons. Certainly the Corporation seemed aware of the need to provide as high a standard of passenger comfort as possible; a concern, one imagines, that would reflect high on the list of priorities reflected in board room minutes.

In the 1930s one did seem to notice an awareness among passengers of the chance of a more comfortable journey on a Stockport car. Waiting for a car on Stockport Road seemed to become mildly speculative game, will it be a Stockport and an easy ride in melodious waltz time, or the merriment of a tango on a Manchester eight wheeler? Indeed, given the choice of a Manchester car at the stop, with a Stockport visible in the distance, the tendency for some passengers might be to wait for the latter vehicle! I know it was a preference shared by my mother and some of her shopping contempories. Never the less, for the real feel of

tramcar riding, well – perhaps the splendid Manchester cars just had that extra bit of 'edge'!

Since there was a strong relationship between Stockport and Manchester in terms of tramways, perhaps a few more words about the latter – and the possible influences that didn't materialise – are relevant here. My own memories of the late 1920s and early 30s of the Manchester Tramways seem to carry a clear impression that this, was an 'aspiring giant', still in process of exciting new development and advancement of the system.

In the early 1920s these were becoming manifest in various ways. The highly imaginative reserved trackways in the centre portion of the impressive new highway extensions of Kingsway and Princess Road, part of Manchester's post war urban development schemes that produced some of the best council housing of this century. One was also aware of impressive new tram depots being built. There were even a few new cars appearing. It did seem part of a new world that held high hopes for the future of the tram system in Manchester – and, possibly, some related systems.

Alas, in respect of the Manchester Tramways, a gradual, unexpected and quite undeserved neglect seemed to materialise. A faltering of vision concerning the developments that might have been, that would lead to, and be the cause of, a swift decline in the later 1930s. A decline that all too quickly revealed a giant reduced to stumbling on feet of clay, the aspirations of the 1920s snuffed out like a light of hope that failed!

Stockport Road, Longsight

101. Stockport Road, Longsight; c.1902. Stockport Road at the junction with Stanley Grove and Dickenson Road. Although the card is postmarked March 1907, I would think that the original photograph from which it was made is much earlier; perhaps 1902/3, especially as there is no evidence in the view of overhead wiring for the 53 route which crossed Stockport Road at this point. The buildings on the left have been demolished and with them some of the character of the old Longsight I remember. Though the building line on the opposite side is still recognisable. Slade Lane 'corner' can still be seen in the distance.

Skirting the flank of Werneth Low on the Long Scenic Ride to Hyde

102. (Left) Mersey Square Depot, c.1946. Car No. 11 standing outside Mersey Square Depot. The route indicator clearly proclaims Hyde to be the destination, which means the photograph will be pre-1st March 1947, since the through service to Hyde ceased after that date. Judging by the long shadows and therefore a low sun, the photograph could have been taken in late autumn and late in the afternoon. So perhaps the car was coming on to an additional rush hour service. *Photo: F.E.J. Ward*

104. (Opposite/right) Bridge Street, 22nd July 1948. At the Tiviot Dale end of Princes Street, car No. 26 has just turned into Bridge Street and is en route to Vernon Park. The tram stop, where it has apparently paused for a moment, can also be seen in the photograph in plate 66, but from an opposite view point. The buildings in the foreground and behind the car, were a familiar feature from this viewpoint until developments in this area during recent years made for considerable change.

The 'Warren Bulkeley' public house, seen to the right of the tram, closed in 1987, and the facade rebuilt around the corner in Bridge street, near the foot of Castle Hill. The Buck and Dog occupied the site of the new Barclays Bank. *Photo: R.J.S. Wiseman*

103. (Below) Princes Street. Car No. 57 has just turned into Princes Street, pausing for a moment before moving towards the initial, short, single track section. Princes Street would, of course, always be quite busy since both the Reddish and the Hyde routes, and other road traffic traversed its length. The buildings and shops that form a backcloth for the tram make quite a contrast to the present day premises that occupy the site! Beneath the newsagents window, a poster advertising a Rugby League match at which the long disbanded Belle Vue Rangers were to entertain St. Helens. *Photo: A.D. Packer*

105. (Below) Bridge Street, c.1949. A view looking down Princes Street in the late 1940s. The street, at least from a point just beyond the front of the tram, has seen little physical change to its facade in the intervening forty odd years leading to the beginning of the 1990s – except for partial pedestrianisation of course. It is the view behind the facade – on both sides, that would now reveal almost undreamed of change to those from previous generations who would still recognise Princes Street as a shopping area. Indeed one wonders how the street survived with so much remaining intact. We are fortunate that so many old roads and 'ways' of similar character survive in our town – long may they remain with us! From the point of view of road traffic – especially as it increased, the restricted nature of Princes Street soon became apparent. It is an indication, I suppose, of its age and the period it emerged from. Thus, apart from a double tramtrack approach at each end and a passing loop near the centre, much of its length was single track. Princes Street was originally part of Heaton Lane, but had it changed in recognition of the visit of the Prince of Wales.

Photo: F.N.T. Lloyd Jones

106. Great Portwood Street, 15th January 1950. The western end of Great Portwood Street on 15th January 1950, with a car making the short run to the Vernon Park terminus. The great bulk of Faulders Mill – only demolished recently in 1989, dominates the background and towers above the last bend of the River Goyt before the latter joins the Tame and together they become the River Mersey. The Queens Hotel – to the right of the car, still survives in a district that, in each direction, has changed almost out of recognition since the above photograph was taken. *Photo: J.H. Meredith*

107. Carrington Road, 15th January 1950. This rather dramatic picture – partly a result of reflected light from damp surfaces – shows car No. 75 about to curve sharp left from Carrington Road into the eastern end of Great Portwood Street. The building on the left is that of St Paul's School. It is a view that is now almost completely unrecognisable – if you discount the area of the gravestones! Whether the present view of roads and traffic *ad nausea*, is to be preferred is a matter of opinion. Well, at least the dog has no problem in crossing the above road! Lincoln Street was straight ahead whilst Brinnington Road commenced to the right behind the telephone kiosk. *Photo: J.H. Meredith*

Vernon Park

When, in March 1947, it was decided to cut the tram route between Edgeley and Hyde back to Vernon Park, its new terminal point came to occupy a stretch of roadway that, in the sense of its topographical surroundings, was and still is most interesting. Looking south from the pavement tram stop one had, and still has, a view of one of Stockports 'green' treasure chests in the form of that priceless – and I mean priceless, asset that is Vernon Park. Trees and greenery in tiered fashion rising gracefully away up the southern edge of the valley.

Now – about turn, and you were confronted by a long row of terraced houses flanked at each end by splendid mill buildings. The mills and houses spanned the neck of a length of the River Goyt stretching in a northerly direction in the form of a long narrow loop. The river also had done an about turn when confronted by a low narrowing ridge which, at that point, still divides two rivers that will eventually meet just a little further to the west and become the one of the famous name. The roadway and tramway crossing the neck of the loop by means of Carrington Bridge and New Bridge.

The area occupied by the mills and houses is now replaced by the rather functional buildings of British Gas and unfortunately, the graceful loop of the river has become somewhat shortened owing to the needs of a motorway route.

LIGHT FIGURES DENOTE A.M. TIMES — DARK FIGURES DENOTE P.M. TIMES

TRAM SERVICES 2, 2a, 2b — **EDGELEY, Dale Street—STOCKPORT, Mersey Square**

	FROM EDGELEY	FROM STOCKPORT
Monday to Friday	5.38, 6.8, 6.25, 6.35, 6.45 a.m. and every 7½ minutes until 11.37 p.m.	5.25, 5.57, 6.15, 6.24, 6.34 a.m. and every 7½ minutes until 11.27 p.m.
Saturday	5.38, 6.8, 6.25, 6.35, 6.45 a.m. and every 7½ minutes until 12.0 noon, then every 5 minutes until 11.30, 11.37 p.m.	5.25, 5.57, 6.15, 6.24, 6.34 a.m. and every 7½ minutes until 12.0 noon, then every 5 minutes until 11.20, 11.27 p.m.
Sunday	1.45, 2.0 p.m. and every 7½ minutes until 11.15, 11.25 p.m.	1.34, 1.49, 2.4 p.m. and every 7½ minutes until 11.4, 11.15 p.m.

TRAM SERVICE 2 — **EDGELEY, Dale Street - HYDE, Town Hall**

Stage No.																			
1	Eogeley, Dale Street																		
2	1	The Armoury																	
3	1	1	Nelson Hotel																
4	1	1	1	St. Petersgate or Mersey Square															
5	1½	1	1	1	Lancashire Bridge														
6	2	2	1½	1	1	St. Paul's Church													
7	2	2	1½	1½	1	1	Vernon Park or Pear Mill												
8	2½	2½	2	1½	1½	1	1	Bredbury Bar											
9	3	3	2½	2	2	1	1	1	Traveller's Call										
10	3	3	2½	2½	2	1½	1	1	1	Bredbury Station									
11	3½	3½	3	2½	2½	2	1½	1½	1	1	St. Mark's Church								
12	4	4	3½	3	3	2	2	2	1	1	1	Woodley Station							
1/13	4½	4½	4	3½	3½	2½	2½	2	1½	1½	1	1	Pole Bank						
2	5	5	4½	4	4	3	3	3	2	2	1½	1	1	Apethorne Lane					
3	5½	5½	5	4½	4½	3½	3½	3	2½	2½	2	1½	1	1	Grapes Hotel				
4	6	6	5½	5	5	4	4	3½	3	3	2½	2	1½	1	1	Werneth Hotel or Mottram Old Road			
5	6	6	5½	5	5	4	4	3½	3	3	2½	2	1½	1	1	1	Cemetery Gates		
6	6½	6½	6	5½	5½	4½	4½	4	3½	3½	3	2½	2	1½	1	1	1	Ring o' Bells	
7	7	7	6½	6	6	5	5	4½	4	4	3½	3	2½	2	2	1½	1	1	Hyde, Town Hall

108. New Bridge Lane, 15th January 1950. That same damp day of 15th January 1950. Though, as this and other photographs of Mr Meredith's in this book prove, a day that may seem disappointing for the photographer, can sometimes provide the sort of atmosphere that makes for a memorable picture. Car No. 75 is ready for the return journey to Edgeley as the conductor repositions the trolley. The view is towards Bredbury, Vernon Park to the right.

Photo: J.H. Meredith

109. New Bridge Lane, 9th April 1949. By way of contrast, to the photograph on the previous page, is this view of Vernon Park terminus looking towards Stockport on 9th April 1949. Obviously a quite different day of sunshine and long shadows. The bus, the rear of which can just be seen behind the tramway pole, will be passing over Carrington Road Bridge. The tram is ready for the return to Edgeley. *Photo: D.F. Tee*

110. Stockport Road, Bredbury. A pre-1914 postcard of Stockport Road, Bredbury adjacent to the Travellers Call. The route was primarily single track but with numerous passing loops, the one at this junction being clearly seen in the photograph. The distant tram would be from the first, No. 1–30 series, of cars, the right hand ascending stairway – a feature of the series, shows very prominently. Doubtless the scenic nature of the route, with good panoramic views on a fine day, would attract passengers to the open upper deck of the car which, on the one in view seems well filled. Ashton Road bears left beyond the Travellers Call.

111. Stockport Road West, Bredbury, c.1912. The buildings in this old postcard view – which I would think to be pre-1914, appear to have changed very little over the passing decades. What makes an interesting focal point for me, is the horse and its small two wheeled cart, plus the little group of – trades people? Faintly seen in the distance is the railway bridge crossing Stockport Road adjacent to Bredbury Station. The double track passing loop leading to single track, continues as single track until well beyond the bridge. The tramway pole on the left appears to have a distinct lean towards the road, which may account for what seems to be a form of support wire. The entrance to Lower Bents Lane is on the right. Coal mining in the Bredbury area is now long forgotten, but the site behind the erring tramway pole was at one time occupied by Bents Pit. It was connected by tramway across the fields to another site in Mill Lane, Woodley.

112. Stockport Road West, Bredbury, 1st March 1947. The date of this photograph, 1st March 1947, was the last day the trams worked through to Hyde. Car No. 4 on the left is proceeding in the direction of Hyde, while car No. 12 is heading towards Stockport. Both cars are standing on the loop adjacent to the junction of Lower Bents Land and Stockport Road, in this view towards Woodley and Hyde.

Photo: R.B. Parr
National Transport Museum

113. Stockport Road East, c.1947. Just the other side of the bridge mentioned in the previous photograph – notice the railway signal partially obscured by the trees – with the tram back on a double track loop. Although the Edgeley–Hyde through route ceased on 1st March 1947 and was cut back to Vernon Park, morning and evening peak period journeys to Bredbury St Marks Church continued until 3rd May 1947 when they too were withdrawn. The above, post war photograph, shows car No. 23 with Edgeley showing on the indicator, so presumably it would be operating to Woodley only. As well as being the stop for Bredbury Station, many local residents will recognise to the right of the tram, the gable end of Alvanley House, latterly the home and surgery for the Milson family practice.

Photo: A.D. Packer

114. Hyde Road, Woodley, 1st March 1947. Another March 1st 1947 photograph, with car No. 26 proceeding to Hyde. The second, from the Stockport direction, of the two low bridges on the Hyde route is seen in the background. It carried the railway lines between Woodley Junction and Tiviot Dale Station. the road begins to rise quite steeply beyond the bridge and, in about 300 yards or so, is crossing over the same section of railway line beyond Woodley Station. That well known local hostelry, the 'White Hart' public house, is to the right beyond the bridge.

Photo: R. Wiseman

115. Woodley Station, 11th September 1961. Stanier 8F 2-8-0 No. 48302 is hauling a train of empty wagons, the brake van of which will be just about passing over the bridge seen in the previous photograph. This line was part of comparatively direct series of routes that linked east and west coasts across the industrial heartland of South Lancashire and Yorkshire. A national asset that has – by stealth, or so it seems to me, been frittered away. Much of it remains in the form of trackbed, but through building on bits of it, here and there, the whole has been destroyed as a long distance route. Woodley Station happily continues to serve Manchester commuter trains. *Photo: R. Keeley*

116. Stockport Road, Hyde. Car No. 21 on the gentle descent past Pole Bank Hall (left), this view emphasising the quite rural appearance at that time, which remains largely to this day, giving a green and leafy atmosphere. The single line leading into the loop and the far end of the loop can just be seen. This was the interchange point for cars that saw brief use in the summer of 1903 – as described in the text. The road at this point becomes Hyde Road as far as Bredbury (George Lane). The subsequent widening here was accommodated by taking land to the left of the picture.

117. Stockport Road, Hyde, c.1906/8. Almost the same viewpoint as that shown below (cf 118) although the several years that separate the two views show some subtle changes in the landscape and make it worthy of inclusion. The Stockport car is one of the first, 1–30, series with the reverse staircase. The lengthy stone wall shows quite clearly that Dowson Road has yet to be built to form the present road junction. Readers may like to pinpoint certain other differences compared to the following view. The date of this scene would be around 1906/08.

118. Stockport Road, Gee Cross, n.d. S.H.M.D. car No. 64 descends from Gee Cross en route from Hyde to Edgeley. The car is adjacent to the junction of Stockport Road and Dowson Road. The blank route number indicator on the balcony guard rail was used when the car operated between Hyde and Manchester, when the route number 19 would be inserted. The view was taken from a series of postcards available from Wadsworths, newsagent in Woodley.

119. Stockport Road, Gee Cross, n.d.
Car No. 18 nearing Gee Cross, the final
stage on its long uphill journey which,
by degrees, has been fairly continuous
from Vernon Park. The Grapes Hotel,
seen in the background, marks the
highest point reached by Stockport
cars, at 517 feet above sea level.

**120. Market Street, Hyde, 12th
August 1937.** Market Street Hyde in
front of the town hall with car No. 63
ready for the return to Edgeley. Much
of the foreground building line remains.
A nostalgic reminder of tramway days
which, to this day, still exists in the
form of an iron framed shelter, can be
seen on the left hand side of the
photograph. It is known that more than
one tram came to grief when travelling
down Market Street, brakes not being
applied in time! *Photo: H.B. Priestley*

121. Market Street, Hyde. A
Stockport car takes passengers aboard
at the terminus in Market Street Hyde.
Hyde Town Hall is on the right Apart
from the joint services operating
between Manchester and Hazel Grove,
Stockport cars shared terminal points
with Manchester cars at both Reddish
and Hyde.

Photo: Stockport M.B. Libraries.

Stockport Road, Hyde.

122. (Left) Hyde Market Street/ Manchester Road, 30th June 1947. So much activity in this view of Manchester corporation bogie car No. 127 about to turn into Market Street for the final couple of hundred yards to the terminus. The overhead wiring for the replacement trolley bus system – which didn't commence until January 16th 1950, is already in place. That service became No. 210 Manchester Piccadilly to Gee Cross. Early post war days, and acute delivery problems for new motor buses, were a cause of lengthy delays before the new trolley buses finally emerged from the Crossley Works. Garbetts shop occupies the site now taken by a slip road to the M67 Hyde By-Pass. *Photo: R.B. Parr, National Transport Museum*

123. (Centre) Stockport Road, Hyde. An interesting view from an old postcard looking towards Hyde as the tram climbs towards Gee Cross. On the left, adjacent to the second tramway pole, can be seen the stone parapet of the railway bridge over the line between Godley and Apethorne Junctions, whilst on the right is the public house known as the Clarkes Arms. The name derives from a Captain Clarke, an early 19th century aristocrat who lived at Hyde Hall and who, I believe, was held high in local esteem.

124. (Bottom Left) Godley Junction, 22nd April 1974. A photograph that, in terms of its relevance to what was a very important rail 'way' through Stockport, is not without significance. The view, at Godley Junction, shows a section of the line between Godley and Apethorne Junctions. At this time, Godley Junction was an important motive power exchange point on a line seeing the passage of very heavy freight trains over the Pennines and through Woodhead Tunnel, from Wath Yards in the Barnsley area. At the junction big diesel locomotives would take over the trains – doubtless similar loads are playing their part in the strain and dislocation suffered by motorway traffic! Parts of this railway are now being frittered away, as can be clearly seen where it passed along the Mersey Valley in the Stockport area. A priceless asset – in national terms, is gradually reduced, and this at a time of great concern about the future of all forms of transport. Take out bits, and the whole, as a through 'way' is immobilised (see caption 115). Surely, as the decades pass, a public – if not government, increasingly concerned and anxious about transport and the environment will ask why – why did it happen?

Having said my piece, a few more details concerning the photograph. The electric locomotives are 76006 and 76008. Brookfold signal box can be seen in the background. In the foreground and somewhat overgrown, are the remains of the old turntable a relic of steam locomotive days. *Photo: R. Keeley*

125. Stockport Road West, Bredbury, c.1947. On our return to Stockport, we come across Car No. 22 at the junction of Stockport Road/ Lower Bents Lane Bredbury, in a similar position to the two cars seen in plate 112 on the same date. A point of interest in this, and the photograph below, is that they illustrate some of the variations in Stockport tram rebuilding over the years. No. 22 retains the right hand ascending staircases – potential head bangers, one would imagine, especially for the taller drivers. The balconies remain open, but the car had 'plant on' vestibules, fitted to the canopy dash and corner pillars in 1928. The two shops to the left of the tram now serve as 'Dry cleaners' and Post Office respectively.

Photo: R.B. Parr,
National Transport Museum

126. New Bridge Lane, 12th March 1950. A busy scene – for those days, at Vernon Park terminus. Car No. 15 ready for the return journey to Edgeley. No. 53 on a special tour of the remaining part of the system on 12th March 1950 (described by Ian Yearsley in his book *The Manchester Tramways*). The position of the Crossley double deck bus in the picture might almost be considered symbolic – overtaking and, perhaps, representing the shadow of the undertaker! Car No. 15 had an extensive rebuild in 1923, after which it emerged from the workshops with fully enclosed top saloons and platforms vestibuled. The front of the dash had a slightly flattened appearance due to the multi radius construction of the platform. I imagine that the wider centre window would also give the driver a better view ahead. Maurice Marshall's indispensable volume on Stockport Tramways explains, in great detail, the construction and rebuilding history of the whole tram fleet. As mentioned previously the houses to the left have made way for the British Gas area offices.

Photo: J. Fozard

127. Stockport. One of a series of picture post cards issued pre-war illustrating five of the town's prominent locations.

To the heart of the Great Cottonopolis

128. Wellington Road North, c.1949. Car No. 82 to the left is on the short run to Crossley Road while car No. 23 is bound for Hazel Grove. This, and the other photographs on this page, were all taken on one day in the late 1940s. The buildings on the right, as far as and beyond the bus, have all been demolished. Heaton Lane Depot Offices, on the left hand side, have also suffered the same fate.
Photo: F.N.T. Lloyd Jones

129. Wellington Road North, c.1949. The photographer has now walked a little further up the hill – Wellington Road North, and has obviously been followed and passed by car No. 82. Some of the buildings are now beginning to look a little more familiar – at least to the 1990s viewer. The Magnet Inn is in the left foreground whilst in the distance, also on the left, is the south facing end wall of the great railway warehouse at Heaton Norris – the same building that carries the legendary name high on the west facing main wall, and clearly seen when travelling by train.
Photo: F.N.T. Lloyd Jones

130. Wellington Road, North, c.1947. Nearing the crest, the photographer paused to snap Car No. 80 on the downward run to Mersey Square. The distant slight hump carries the main road across Belmont Bridge, below which are the railway lines that, having left the main line at Heaton Norris Junction, head towards Reddish and Guide Bridge. At this point the buildings are little changed, as seen by todays viewer. Most prominent of course being the Hope Inn, seen in right foreground. *Photo: F.N.T. Lloyd Jones*

131. Wellington Road North/Heaton Moor Road, c.1949. In January 1949 the last remaining tramway route into Manchester (No. 35) was withdrawn, and replaced between Hazel Grove and Piccadilly Manchester by bus service No. 92. However, for the next twelve months, Stockport trams still operated a service, alongside the buses, between Crossley Road and Hazel Grove, the tram route finally being withdrawn in January 1950.

This photograph, taken on the same day as the three on the previous page, shows the junction of Heaton Moor Road and Wellington Road North, with car No. 82 on the return service to Hazel Grove. Apart from the demolition – many years ago, of the large house, in the right foreground, the view is identifiable with that of today, just!

Photo: F.N.T. Lloyd Jones

132. Wellington Road North, c.1949. Car No. 6 is standing just south of Crossley Road and, judging by its almost totally empty appearance, is probably on a short working from Stockport. In the right foreground, behind the wall, can be seen part of the buildings of what was known as Blackbrook Farm. In this area, a section of the stream, known as the Black – or Cringle, Brook can still be seen weaving its sinuous way behind houses, small factories and through parkland that takes the name Cringle from the Brook. In the background to the left is the building that, as a boy, I would know as the Tramway Offices. Beyond here in the Manchester direction, the A6 takes on the name of Stockport Road (Levenshulme).

Photo: F.E.J. Ward

133. Stockport Road, 1st March 1947. Lloyd Road on the right with a corner of the Tramway Offices, built in 1926, in view. These offices replaced similar facilities at Levenshulme, when the loop line at the latter point was removed and the Lloyd Road siding came into use. Manchester bogie car No. 1053 is on the No. 35 service Hazel Grove–Manchester Exchange. The Stockport car in the background, is probably en route to Hazel Grove. Photographed March 1st 1947. The houses to the left are on Cringle Road.

Photo: R.B. Parr,
National Transport Museum

134. Stockport Road, Levenshulme, c.1906. A view in the opposite direction to the one in the old postcard depicted in plate 99. This one – with a new year greeting written on the reverse of the card, is postmarked 1906; at which time the coming of the electric tramcar itself would be a fairly recent and momentous happening for the young ladies in the foreground. But a tramcar with a top cover that was almost brand new – no more travelling 'on top' in the rain, that was quite an event!

135. Stockport Road, Longsight. Another old postcard view to compare with the one shown in plate 101. This one, postmarked 1908, shows the junction of Stockport Road and Stanley Grove. The view is now completely different, all the buildings are now long demolished – yet, if you were to about turn at this spot today, you would find the building line on the opposite side of the road very little changed. The destination board on the open top tram clearly reads Stockport. In the foreground the lady on the bicycle – doubtless confident in the slow pace of the traffic, rides diagonally and nonchalantly across the tram lines.

136. Plymouth Grove, Longsight, c.1927. The style of dress being worn by the two ladies on the left in the photograph, suggested that this is a mid 1920s view of Plymouth Grove, Longsight. The junction with Upper Brook Street shows faintly in the distance. Manchester bogie car No. 952 – then fairly new, having been built 1925/26, is on one of the joint services between Stockport and Manchester; the 35.B operating between Mersey Square and Albert Square, Manchester. Notice the motor cycle combination, wheels strategically positioned to avoid getting stuck in the tram lines.

Photo: Edward Gray

137. London Road, Manchester, n.d. Difficult to exactly date this old postcard view since there is no postmark on the back; though the proliferation of those magical letters L & N.W.R., on posters and station sign boards, suggest it to be pre the railway grouping of 1923.

Dominating the background is a magnificent building, whose majestic and dignified appearance gave, in the past, distinction to the station approach. Soot encrusted no doubt, but, had it survived, how superb it would have looked if cleaned. Though the station was owned by the London & North Western Railway, the Great Central Railway did have a foothold – albeit only three platforms, as joint operator of services out of the station.

The tram is Manchester bogie car No. 549, en route to Heaton Chapel from Victoria Street. It was one of a series of double deck cars that were the first to receive top covers in 1904/5. The graceful appearance of the covers brought to these cars the almost rhapsodic name of 'Balloons'!

138. Manchester: Piccadilly/London Road. Pre 1914 view from the corner of Piccadilly looking towards London Road Station. Apart from a couple of horse drawn carts and Car No. 563 – one of the 'Balloons' as mentioned elsewhere, there is no traffic to view. There is still a familiar look to the building line on the left, though the elegant Queens Hotel, on the right, was demolished in the early 1970s and replaced by a rather less than elegant office block. Names of one time well known shipping lines – Union Castle, North German Lloyd etc, appear on the near buildings on the left adding to the nostalgia of the view. Lloyds Bank nowadays occupy the building to the left.

139. Piccadilly, Manchester, c.1948. With the shape of things to come on each side, Stockport car No. 54 pauses, far from home, in George Street, Manchester Piccadilly. The photograph dates from 1948 when, for a short period – February 1948 to January 8th 1949, Stockport cars operated and extended version of the 35C route, between Hazel Grove and Piccadilly. I suppose it could be considered to represent part of the final death throes of the Manchester Tramway system. Littlewoods department store occupies the taller building to the right which formerly served as the Piccadilly Cinema. (cf 152). *Photo: F.E.J. Ward*

140. Albert Square, Manchester, 4th April 1947. Stockport car No. 60 standing in Albert Square Manchester on April 4th 1947. The car is on the 35B service, which operated between Stockport St Peters Square and Albert Square. Manchester's decision to introduce one way traffic systems in June 1938, produced further complications to an already complex tramway system in the city centre. From the above date the 35B, on the inward journey, turned left out of Upper Brook Street into Grosvernor Street, then right into Oxford Street, proceeding via Peter Street/Mount Street into Albert Square; returning, as previously, via Princess Street. The tram route was finally converted to bus operation on February 16th 1948.

Since the close up view of the tram rather obscures the buildings, except for a part of the Albert Memorial and the town hall extension – the latter completed in May 1938, I am including two further views of the Square from old postcards.   *Photo: J. Fozard*

141. Albert Square, Manchester, n.d. From the corner of Lloyd Street/Mount Street, this is what I believe to be a late 'Edwardian' period view of Albert Square. The buildings are a little hazy, thought the sunshine seems to have nicely highlighted the 'traffic' and the people. Seen above the handcart is a four wheeled Manchester car, top covered but open balcony and platform. The line up of Hansom cabs, awaiting prospective customers, certainly enhance the 'period' atmosphere of the picture. Of further interest is the way the photographer has allowed the tramlines to dominate the foreground. Perhaps he was trying to give emphasis to what would still be a comparatively new age of transport.

A Favourite 'Way'

Life, and living, you take it as it comes. But the way it affects the individual is dependant on the basic inborn emotional nature of the character. And surely, to some degree, it is a matter of being in the right place at the right time, and making the best of it.

For those of us with an interest in tramcars and railways – and for me the two did go together, the mid 1930s was and enthralling time. My good luck was that it coincided with my mid teens, when trams appeared to have reached a zenith both in variety, shape and appeal, or so it seemed to me. Sadly though, the evidence that it was a dying phase in Britain was becoming all too obvious. On the railways, superb pre-grouping steam locomotives were still very much in evidence as they inter-mingled with exciting new designs springing to life from the fertile imagination of great engineers and, in due course, they would immortalise the names of Gresley and Stanier.

Oh lucky me! To have all this plus the sort of job I had set my heart on. Fortune had served me well. Any artistic talent I possessed was being developed through an apprenticeship in the Artists Department, C.W.S. Printing Works, Longsight.

It was a time when I frequently travelled into Manchester on the tram and usually on one of the Stockport–Manchester routes. Sometimes it would be just for the ride of perhaps on errand for one of the three journeymen with whom I worked, and that might be in my lunch hour when I could just about make the return trip before 'clocking on'! On every occasion, whatever the purpose, there was always the thrill and pleasure of the ride; but, it must be admitted, there were times when a special reason for the journey would be uppermost in my mind. The icing on the cake so to speak – as you will later deduce!

Stockport Road, Longsight, always had an air of vigour and importance, with three major tramway junctions, bustling shops and people, three cinemas, the inevitable public houses and, it seemed, always a tram in sight. Waiting for the tram brought the usual conflicting aspects of 'choice' – much like it is on T.V. when the two programmes we want to see are screened at the same time and the word becomes a contradiction! In this case there was a double problem. To wait for a particular type of tram and operator, or go for a particular route, which could be, Piccadilly, Victoria Street or Albert Square dependant on whether or not it was a leisure ride. So hard to choose, since each route, by virtue of their inter-connecting with other routes, could provide a veritable feast for the observer. However – and by a very narrow margin be it said, the route via Plymouth Grove to Albert Square seemed destined to become a prime favourite.

This favourite 'way', as recollected from impressions carried on the rim of youthful memory by this rather serious sixteen/seventeen year old, produces a tangle of thoughts and emotions. A mixture of nostalgia for the past, a feeling for place, and a degree of looking forward. But was he peering through rose tinted spectacles? Well, possibly, yet those impressions did appear to carry something of the optimism of youth, of hope that 'things will get better'. A feeling that seemed to be reflected by ones elders, where an optimism prevailed despite hard times.

As the tram veered at the junction of Plymouth Grove and Stockport Road we appeared, almost immediately, to enter and progress through an area of fragile leafy charm, a quite different locality compared to the busy area we have just left behind. For a few moments one could have imagined, illogically perhaps, that we

142. Albert Square, Manchester, c.1920. Again from the southern end of the square, it is interesting to compare this view with that seen on the previous page, particularly as this one probably dates from ten to fifteen years later. The most striking difference is the replacement of the Hansom cabs by a primitive but elegant collection of motor vehicles. Certainly a transformation of the 'taxi rank'! One of the very attractive 'Balloon' cars (see plate 137) can be seen in the background, carrying route indication number 12 which, I believe, would be Hightown to Chorlton at that time, and one of the totally enclosed cars, that gave later additions to the fleet the distinctive 'Manchester look', (see plates 35 & 55) can be seen to the left of the Albert Memorial; with two more enclosed cars to the right in the picture. A clue to the dating of the picture – the enclosed form of cars did not appear in any number until the beginning of the 1920s.

were heading towards a more rural environment instead of the city centre. It has to do, I suppose, with towns and cities ever expending outward, but leaving some areas little changed from the time when they represented the outer edges, a process that seems to have continued throughout the past century down to our present age.

Progressing along Plymouth Grove, one is soon conscious that the edge of Victoria Park, with its elegant and spacious houses, is never far away. The structures remain but appear to rest in the shadow of the one time affluent society who created them, and who are themselves now part of the chronicles of a different era.

There quickly follows, and in close up, a most distinctive and benign of appearance dwelling from another age. Indeed, this one, though endowed with a past, seems possessed of a 'presence'. Or is it my imagination again? For this is the one time home of Elizabeth Gaskell which the tram, with gentle rocking grace of movement is gliding past.

Then, with a shuddering little wriggle, we are across the junction where Plymouth Grove meets Upper Brook Street, and immediately aware of the stern but faded grandeur of a rather different kind of Victorian housing. Some, of the terraced variety, others standing slightly more aloof behind small gardens and grandiose entrance ways. Doubtless a district that would claim to have Victorian lower middle class origins but now somewhat shrouded in the mists of time. Long past, its morning of Spring when the area was no great distance from green fields and farmland

and more akin to outer suburban than inner city. Such a prospect would be difficult to imagine, even in the 1930s!

Onward along Princess Street and, as we cross, with rumbustious clatter, two sets of intersecting double tracks, a glimpse along Whitworth and Portland Streets to where, in each direction, the great warehouses are assembled in close ranks; appearing to stand shoulder to shoulder in a kind of authoritarian majesty, proclaiming, or so it would seem, something of Manchester industrial prowess.

I would see them as representing the prelude – the overture to the scenic spectacle that follows; an imaginary curtain rising as the car, after crossing Moseley Street, takes the curve into the dignified setting of Albert Square. A panorama of fine buildings on all sides, with a centre piece formed by the elegant memorial to Prince Albert and other statues raised in memory of men held high in local esteem. A marvellous backcloth to the building that rises above all. Indeed, it could be described as the jewel in the crown of Manchester's great Victorian buildings, the superb Town Hall!

So, was the preference for the route related to a naive boyish sense of successful ventures and getting on in the world? Or could it have been a different but interlinked emotion that occasionally surfaced? Well, whatever the answer to the first question, there is no doubt that an emphatic YES, answers the second! For, and dare I whisper it, there was another equally elegant building though
continued over

143. Manchester, Oxford Road, c.1906. July 1907. That is the post mark on the reverse of the postcard and indeed the view will date from about that time. The car in the foreground, No. 160, is a four wheeled open topper one of a series (107–187) built 1901/02. In the distance, among a little group of cars, is one of the early top covered cars known as 'Balloons', it would then be comparatively brand new. Clearly seen in the centre, to the left of the car, is the superb ornate frontage of the old Hippodrome Theatre. This and buildings adjacent were later replaced by the more austere frontage of a cinema. In the far distance can be seen the tower of St Peters Church, the church opening in 1794 with the tower being added in 1816. Both were demolished in 1907. Oxford Road became part of the one way system which, in June 1938, was used by cars on the 35B service on their inward journey to Albert Square. Great Bridgewater Street is the first street to the left of the picture.

THE HIPPODROME & OXFORD ROAD, MANCHESTER.

moulded to a rather different shape, and, as one might say, just a stones throw from the 'Square'.

This vast semi circular cavern had a mesmeric effect on me; for it seemed to be forever beckoning and once lured in its direction I became spellbound. Not that the modest entrance way gave any real indication of the transformation that awaited within and so quick to captivate me with sights and sound that were both music to the ears and a visual delight.

The immediate greeting might be a great gusty roar of steam exhaust that, in a slow march of hollow drum beats, reverberated around the vast semi enclosed space. Or the shrill piping of a steam whistle, soon lost in a multitude of shimmering echoes, setting, as one might imagine, a myriad patterning of glass panels a-tingling. Then the sudden burst of a safety valve lifting – and equally sudden to silence. The occasional melifluous hiss of simmering steam – the quiet glide of the bow across strings.

The sounds are an indication of the sights, for this great hall of echoes played host to the most graceful figuring in steel imaginable. The same that with their vibrant living presence, captivated and compelled my attention.

Some, endowed with a breathtaking beauty, were, and indeed remain – but now in black and white photographs, a feast for my eyes. In particular, the elegant Midland Compounds – and elegance was there in every curving line including the graceful swing of coupling/connecting rods; a clue perhaps to their fond though unofficial title 'Crimson Ramblers'. Competing for attention were the larger, ex Great Central 4-6-0s which radiated power, vitality, and strength of sinew, even when at rest. And one could go on.

Well may I call the tram route 35B a favourite 'way', even though dilemma could follow in its wake. A happy dilemma – if one may use an apparent contradiction, since the choice, tramcars in abundance and variety in Albert Square and, it seemed, in which every direction you moved; and of course, steam trains in Central Station – the mind boggled!

For me, it was a wonderful world and although I didn't realise it at the time, the next couple of decades or so, despite – or perhaps because of, the intervention of war, would provide some of my most endearing and enduring memories of trams, trains, and travel throughout Britain.

144. Manchester Central, 5th April 1957. 'Superb Midland Compounds for me to feast my eyes on' – but that was in the mid 1930s! This view was photographed 'twenty odd' years later, after an abundance of feasting such as I would never in my wildest dreams have expected in these earlier days. Now, in the later 1950s, the trams had mostly departed this life; though the steam locomotive scene still had much to offer – but it was rapidly diminishing. Midland Compound 41118 – all sombre innocence compared to the fiery mood seen earlier in the book (caption No. 65) when I had travelled behind her from Manchester Central to Tiviot Dale Station. The engine was built in 1925, at a time when Derby still had a dominating influence on the locomotive design policy on what had become Britain's largest railway – The London Midland & Scottish; and was not scrapped until early 1958. According to her driver, with whom I chatted after taking the photograph, she had recently emerged ex works from a major overhaul, though over 30 years of age. He thought this was due to the soundness of her frames. But even so, she only had a few months to go.
Photo: R. Keeley

145. Manchester, Midland Hotel, c.1915. Post stamped 1916. The magnificent Midland Hotel designed by George Trubshaw for the Midland Railway Company. Building commenced in 1898 and on being opened in 1904 it could boast a Palm Court, Winter Gardens, Concert Hall and Theatre, French and Italian Restaurants, as well as 400 bed chambers. Sad that the temporary looking wooden entrance ways to the station that lasted throughout its life, could not have matched the grand style of the hotel and the great semi-circular train shed, as happened at the other end of the line at St Pancras.

Midland Hotel, Manchester.

A Galaxy of Tramcars

One of the most important tramway routes that saw Stockport cars operating alongside those formidable double bogie giants from Manchester, was also the most direct 'way' between Mersey Square and Piccadilly/Exchange, Manchester. Appropriately, for much of its length it was, and still is, just plain Stockport Road. In using the route, you may have travelled from the most southerly point on the map visited by a Stockport car – or a Manchester one for that matter, Hazel Grove; to the most northerly plain graced by a Stockport car, Manchester Exchange. There were two terminal points for Stockport cars, one in George Street, Piccadilly, the other at that fascinating meeting place of tramways, railways and riverway opposite Manchester Cathedral.

Therefore I thought this little grouping of tram and tramway scenes in the heart of Manchester would be of interest to all of us who feel an affinity with this North West region.

CATHEDRAL AND EXCHANGE STATION, MANCHESTER

147. Cathedral and Exchange Station, c.1921. A panoramic view of the Exchange terminus from an early 1920s postcard. The Exchange Station building on the left, would become a victim of the December 23rd 1940 air raid. The Manchester car in the foreground is on the No. 32 route to Reddish.

146. (Above) Victoria Street, Manchester, December 1946. As can be seen from the photograph, the Exchange was a terminus for more than one service. Manchester car No. 163 – on the No. 19 route to Hyde, was from the last series of cars that were known as the Pilchers, the name deriving from that of the General Manager of the system R. Stuart Pilcher. Since he favoured the development of the bus as a replacement for the trams, his name finds little favour with tramway enthusiasts, though doubtless his intentions were an attempt to resolve – in the way he thought best at the time, the growing problem of increased traffic and congestion in the city. I believe that hindsight shows him to be mistaken – but of course that is the advantage of hindsight! Stockport car No. 83, operating on route 35 Exchange–Hazel Grove, awaits its turn to move forward to the crossover, which the Stockport car in the background is about to use.

Photo: R.B. Parr,
National Transport Museum

148. Victoria Street, Manchester, c.1945. The pale shadow behind car 985 is part of the Exchange Station train shed; an intentionally apt description, since, with the destruction of its fine entrance way and office building in the December 1940 blitz, something of its former distinctive presence had already departed. The station approach sign boards proclaim its then, mid-1940s, London Midland & Scottish Railway ownership. Stockport car No. 47 prepares to move back to the crossover, while the Manchester car – Hazel Grove on the indicator, is awaiting to make the same manoeuvre. The photograph giving the two cars something of a David and Goliath appearance! Behind the camera, Victoria Street continued in a westerly direction to become Deansgate.

Photo: J. Fozard

Carrying Money is dangerous; Have your purchases sent home by "Tram," and pay on delivery.

SHOP BY TRAM––
It gives you the choice of district.

149. Victoria Street, Manchester, c.1937. Each patiently awaiting their turn! Stockport car No. 76 appears to 'buffer up' to the Manchester 'Pilcher' car. One of Manchester's older school of design – on the No. 19 route to Hyde, prepares to move over the crossover, a move being apparently closely observe by intending passengers, seen to the right of the Stockport car, in this early 1947 view. The Pilchers – more officially known as the Pullmans, gave, in my experience, a most comfortable ride. Fifty odd years ago they might have been seen as a portend of things to come. Instead, they became the last modern design of tramcar to operate in the Greater Manchester area.

Photo: R.J.S. Wiseman

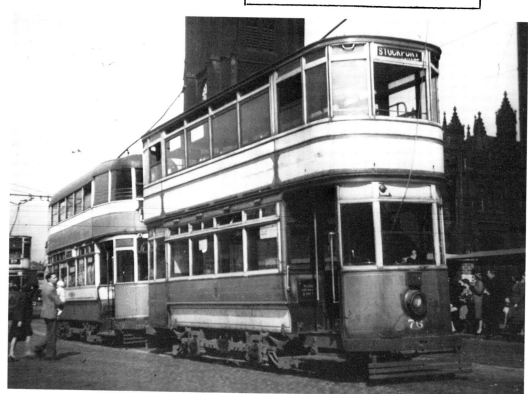

150. Victoria Street, Manchester, c.1925. A mid 1920s view, but now changed almost out of recognition. The great central edifice, known as the Victoria Buildings and which incorporated the Victoria Hotel, was completed in 1878. It was destroyed in the December blitz of 1940. Post war developments have brought further great changes, though the way through towards Deansgate, on the right, still remains. The tram on the left is en route to Hazel Grove, while that on the right shows route 32 indicating Reddish as its destination. First it will need to traverse the crossover – the latter being crossed, at that moment, by the small dog in charge of the two ladies!

151. Victoria Street, Manchester, c.1946. An early post war view with the Victoria Buildings now just a memory, although allowing greater prominence to Cromwell's statue. The latter was moved to Wythenshawe Park in 1968. Each of the trams in the photograph has a slightly careworn appearance – almost as if there is an awareness that the end is nigh!

Photo: J. Fozard

152. Piccadilly, Manchester, c.1935. Since the Piccadilly cinema is advertising a Shirley Temple film 'Stand Up and Cheer', made in 1934, the date of this old postcard is clearly about 1935. The view is across the north westerly end of Piccadilly with George Street in the foreground. The side on buildings to the left – destroyed in the December 1940 bombing, separated George Street from Moseley Street, forming a V shape after which the two streets meet towards the middle left in the photograph. George Street, over the years, had been the terminus for a few different routes; including the final extended version of the 35C route between Piccadilly and Hazel Grove, operated by Stockport cars. The Manchester car in the foreground is, as far as I can make out, No. 762, built 1913/14; route number and destination showing as 39A Fog Lane.

153. Piccadilly, Manchester, c.1946. George Street again, but no longer clearly separated from Moseley Street. A post war view with Manchester car No. 618 preparing for a short run to Levenshulme Lloyd Road. With the development of the Piccadilly Plaza area and the bus station, this end of George Street virtually ceased to exist – though the shape of the gardens at this end does present a clue!

Photo: J. Fozard

Ring the Funeral Bell

Sadly, and inconceivably the dawn of the 1930s saw a beginning of the twilight period for tramways in Britain, and by the end of the decade the rot had well and truly set in. Ironically the first half of the next decade with its wartime restrictions brought reprieve to what remained of some systems. But the decline was well advanced and the bones of many a skeleton, the last remnants of what might have been, were, towards the end of the 1940s, nearing a point of disintegration.

In Stockport, valiant efforts were made to maintain the efficiency of the tramways but abandonment of the system became a foregone conclusion, especially after the final heart aching end of the Manchester system came at the close of 1948. Operations on remaining routes within the Stockport boundary struggled on for a time after joint operation with Manchester and S.H.M.D. had ceased with the closure of those tramways. Then final abandonment in Stockport came on 25th August 1951 – fifty years after inauguration of the electric tramways. Thus Stockport did have a last word, in that the operation of tramways in the town had continued after all others in the Greater Manchester area had ceased. A distinction, but, unfortunately, a rather hollow one.

In some towns and cities strenuous efforts were made to fit the tram into the post war transport scene; notably, in my own experience, Sheffield. The new trams introduced by Sheffield Corporation Tramways in 1950/52 were modern in appearance, smooth running, fast, and very comfortable to ride in and, of vital importance, they operated on superbly maintained track. One could have hoped this would be the beginning of a new era for the tram in that the city but alas, it was not to be.

The people responsible for the rejuvenation and modernisation of public transport in early post war Britain seemed quite unable to visualise the many advantages and future possibilities inherent in the tramcar, especially with its controlled and economical use of land where it concerns the trackway space required compared to other vehicles of the road. Its capacity to move people en masse, with the minimum use of the earth's resources to create its motive power. Control, the word is significant, in terms of movement, safety, organisation, economy, etc. And yet those far sighted visionaries of the 1920s, who conceived Manchester's Kingsway and Princess Parkway with their reserved tramways, had long ago made a valid point, for that indeed was a first stage that could have seen expansion and development. But the possibilities in Manchester and elsewhere, Sheffield, Liverpool, Leeds etc, where reserved track or other improvements to the system had been made

continued over

154. Mersey Square Depot, 12th March 1950. Emerging briefly into the light of day, like a grey apparition from another age, is works car No. 101. The date Sunday 12th March 1950, shortly after a group of enthusiasts had arrived in Mersey Square Depot in their tour car No. 53, to find a rather special bonus for their cameras to focus on. No. 101 had started life almost half a century earlier as car No. 26 from the first batch of cars (1–30) built for Stockport Corporation Tramways, a car that had remained an 'open topper' but, in the early 1920s became used as a breakdown vehicle. In the mid 1920s it was properly equipped with a bench and other repair facilities after the seating had been removed. Steel rung ladders replaced the reversed staircases, the car being painted in battleship grey and renumbered 101 about four years later. In company with other remaining cars in the fleet, it was finally withdrawn in August 1951. The ominous presence of the buses – a Crossley double decker – is prominent on the left, seems to be a portend. The final sounding of that knell will not be long delayed!

Photo: J. Fozard

in those earlier decades, appear to have been totally unobserved by transport officials in high places.

Ironically, the very routes in Manchester where this pointer to future to future development had first been made, were, twenty years later, the places to experience tramway travel at its worst. The rough riding of the magnificent Manchester bogie cars along Kingsway in the 1940s, was, at times, a quite frightening experience. They jolted, rocked, and swayed in a most alarming way, giving the impression that the tramcar was just a clumsy dangerous contraption. At times one imagined it as an intentional mockery, a stifling of those with vision, a way of persuading a travelling public that this was a decrepit system we needed to be rid of.

It all seemed indicative of a pathetic disinterest in this mode of transport throughout the country. How different to the way tramways continued to develop in many towns and cities on the European Continent where, in contrast to ourselves, out of the ashes of war came renewed and developing systems.

Now, nearly half a century later, our transport 'powers that be' have, it seems, awakened to the potential of light rapid transport railed systems. An irony indeed – especially if you consider 'what might have been' had the last half century seen a continuing development of our tramways, possibly as an integral part of modern road systems. Our weakness is underlined by those two words 'continuing development'!

As I see it, we in Britain are stuck in a lengthy rut of indecision in high places. Perhaps it is the price we pay for out democratic system of government which, admirable though it may be in many respects, does not appear capable of committing us – irrespective of party, though doubtless due in some degree to the machinations of party politics, to long term planning for our public transport systems. Thus we have what could be described as a form of stop-go piecemeal development, coupled with a public versus private ownership tug of war. Together, and with the addition of financial constraints, they seem set fair to continue making an 'aunt sally' of public transport.

In the meantime a glory of this world has passed into oblivion, for whatever the future holds in store, it is unlikely that will ever again see vehicles on rail to match the variety, colour, and style of the tramcar of yesterday, and certainly nothing to match the inherent elegance, the charisma, that appeared to radiate from every shapely curve and panel!

155. Heaton Lane, 14th May 1949. Not quite the end of the system, but near enough! Unidentified car, but possibly one of the 45-50 series, turning into Heaton Lane Depot. This series were eventually all labelled with the double H.H. identifying them as low bridge cars. There is, for me, something almost symbolic about the above photograph, a sort of 'home to roost' flavour, especially as none of the trams had long to go.

Photo: courtesy A.D. Packer

156. London Road, Hazel Grove; 9th January 1949. Special tour cars 74 & 67 pause at Hazel Grove terminus on 9th January 1949. A kind of celebration of the 35 route between Manchester Exchange and Hazel Grove, though rather a sad one since it was the last day of operation for the Manchester cars. After the tour, Mr Ian Yearsley and friends made the last journey between the two points on Manchester car No. 940. The journey being vividly yet poignantly described in his Manchester Tramways book. This view is towards Stockport from the Macclesfield Road direction.

Photo: J. Fozard

Another glance – around yesterday's corner

157. Wellington Road North, c.1909. Though the gradual slope of Wellington Road North is familiar enough in this early postcard view, the building line has changed considerably over the passing years. The tramlines can be seen curving both into Mersey Square and, what was then Heaton Lane, the latter being renamed Princes Street after the visit of the Prince and Princess of Wales on July 6th 1908, primary reason of which being the official opening of the new town hall. The open top Manchester car will no doubt be travelling via Mersey Square and Dawbank to St Peters Square, returning via St Petersgate and Wellington Road South along the single track seen on the left. The gasholder structure, seen on the left, occupies the site that was eventually used for the building of Heaton Lane Tram Depot, the latter opening in January 1924.

158. Wellington Road North, March 1947. An interesting photographic contrast to the above old postcard view, with something like forty years separating them. The changes in the building line will be fairly obvious, although now, another forty years on the change in the view, compared to either of the above, is almost total! The tram, No. 75, is on service to Reddish. Note the policeman on point duty just to the right of the car. It would certainly be a brave man who would stand in the centre of a road junction to direct todays – sometimes aggressive, traffic! *Photo: F.N.T. Lloyd Jones*

159. Mersey Square, c.1935/36. The above postcard view probably dates from 1935/6. The first section of Merseyway – the covering of the river between Wellington Road arches and the eastern side of the old Mersey Bridge, has been completed and the resultant road widening is clear to see. Most of the buildings that can be seen have, with one or two exceptions, been demolished. The transport also now finds a place in the appropriate history books – the three North Western single deck buses in the foreground and, of course, both of the tram cars. An interesting feature of the picture, which of course would be quite out of place today, are the many smoking chimneys!

160. Horse and Farrier, Gatley, c.1908. The westward extension of the tracks at Gatley, with the fields and farms of North Cheshire just a few minutes walk away. Car No. 21, with the right hand ascending staircase, shows the return destination Reddish on the indicator. The tram driver chats nonchalantly to a local – in the middle of the road! The driver is wearing protective rainwear, very necessary when standing in such an exposed wintry – note the trees are without leaf–driving position. The track is in fact a passing loop leading to the final, single, terminal section, seen in the foreground.

161. St Peters Square, c.1908.
Another old postcard view of St Peters Square. The top covered Stockport car (the first top covered series 41–45 were delivered in 1906) preparing to return to Hazel Grove, makes an interesting contrast to the open top Manchester car No. 430, on the right. The latter (from a series of four wheeled cars build 1901/03) displays Piccadilly on the destination board. To the left of the top covered car is an open top Stockport car with the reversed Staircase – I think the number might be 15. It will probably be en route to Edgeley. Of interest, in the right foreground, is the horse cab and cabbies and behind them their little waiting room.

162. Mersey Square, March 1947.
This – for several reasons, is a most interesting photograph. The two cars are from the original 1–30 batch. Car No. 30 was originally No. 1 and as such had remained in open top form. Then, in 1927, it came out of passenger service and found use in various ways as a general repairs and maintenance vehicle. In 1941 it received a repaired top cover removed from car No. 39. The latter, a high bridge car, had been inadvertently booked for the Hyde route and became jammed under the railway bridge at Bredbury in January 1941, causing considerable damage to the top cover. Before fitting the top cover to No. 1 (it wasn't renumbered 30 until February 1944) it was strengthened with additional window pillars – the reason for the six side windows. It remained open balcony but had 'plant on' vestibules.

Car No. 24 received low bridge top covers in 1921 and 'plant on' vestibules in 1938. It may be an optical illusion, but the difference in height between No. 30 and its high bridge top cover, and No. 24, does seem to show.

The ornate clock above the roof of the Mersey Square tram offices indicates the time as ten to five, which would suggest that the two cars are on short run rush hour services. Car No. 30 is standing on what was known as the siding, the crew apparently waiting for their turn to move towards Wellington Road North.

Photo: F.N.T. Lloyd Jones

163. Wellington Road North, c.1949.
Car No. 23 standing just beyond the crossover a few yards up Wellington Road North from Heaton Lane corner. After the trolley pole has been reversed, it will be on the short run back to Dialstone Lane. The car was fitted with a low bridge top cover after the 1914/18 war, the balconies and platforms being vestibuled during a partial rebuild in 1928. The building in the immediate background have all been demolished, although doubtless many local people will remember the timber yard that features behind the three wheeled motor cycle 'van'.

Photo: F.E.J. Ward

A Final Curtain

164. (Above) 165. (Below), Princes Street, 25th August 1951. The very last day of tramcar operation in Stockport. After the Cheadle Heath service was withdrawn on April 10th 1951, the only remaining route, to Reddish, used Princes Street – adjacent to Brown Street, as a terminal point. The three rather evocative photographs taken by Mr D. Packer, two on this page and one on the back cover, seem to capture a mood of celebration, although that is possibly a figment of my imagination. It is perhaps more likely that the presence of people and trams in such crowded profusion, is coincidental to the presence of a tramway terminal point in the towns, rather narrow, main shopping street, on a busy Saturday afternoon. However, we can perhaps daydream a little, and see the crowds as representing a commemoration – a salute for the passing of a noble workhorse that, for half a century, served the town so well.

Photos: A.D. Packer